KITCHEN WITCHERY
for Everyday Magic

KITCHEN WITCHERY
for Everyday Magic

Bring Joy and Positivity
into Your Life with Restorative Rituals
and Enchanting Recipes

REGAN RALSTON
Creator of Water of Whimsy

PAGE STREET
PUBLISHING CO.

PAGE STREET
PUBLISHING CO.

Copyright © 2023 Regan Ralston

First published in 2023 by
Page Street Publishing Co.
27 Congress Street, Suite 1511
Salem, MA 01970
www.pagestreetpublishing.com

Distributed by Macmillan, sales in Canada by The Canadian Manda Group.

27   26   25   24   23   1   2   3   4   5

ISBN-13: 978-1-64567-903-5
ISBN-10: 1-64567-903-9

Library of Congress Control Number: 2022947379

Cover and book design by Meg Baskis for Page Street Publishing Co.
Illustrations by Regan Ralston

Printed and bound in United States

DEDICATION

To Nana, for teaching me about the fairies and
putting a paintbrush in my hand.

Contents

Meeting the Witch of Whimsy

Wild cicadas sing their deep-throated song of summer where yellow grass grows high and dry from an unrelenting sun. In the distance, a pond ripples with fertile movement, framed by cattails and one large weeping willow, which almost appears as if it's bending down gracefully for a look into some murky green mirror. This is the view from my tiny studio window, situated in the A-frame upstairs of a little cabin lost among the hills of upstate New York. I wanted to share this view with you to express the way in which my mind wanders. Some might say this is daydreaming run amok, but I believe my tendency toward verse, fantasy and observation of the everyday is what makes life truly magical.

In much of my work, I've referred to myself as "The Witch of Whimsy," a moniker that meshed perfectly when paired with the name of my art studio, "Water of Whimsy." The key element of these titles being an emphasis on "whimsy." Doesn't that word just roll off the tongue? Say it silently to yourself, whim-sy, a whim that has taken itself off on wings and darted into the night. To me, whimsy reflects that tendency I identify in myself, this habit of seeing and making more than rests squarely in reality. Whimsy is a vehement commitment to daydreaming, to magic-making, to imagination. Whimsy can be like a spiritual guide, at times, driving me toward a meditation on the shape of a hummingbird's wing or the feeling of a fall breeze as it tickles my shoulders. While whimsy itself appears as an ephemeral thing, it is the harnessing of this element that allows for all my grandest creations and experiences.

The term "Witch" then, as it relates to "Witch of Whimsy," refers to my own practice crafting magic from the everyday. It is through a connection with whimsy that I bring beauty and joy into existence; sometimes this appears as a creation of artwork, other times as a tea party hosted for some coterie of mermaids. I want to specify now: My use of the term Witch is in no way imaginary or fanciful. While much of my personal relationship to witchcraft is full of whimsy and everyday magic, I also acknowledge that there are many paths of the craft that may appear as diverse as flowers in a field. I honor and respect the title of Witch as adopted by those who are practitioners of magic in every sense of the word. Of my personal relationship to magic, I identify with the realms of the craft centered within the home. Long before I adopted the title of Witch, my husband would lovingly refer to my cooking as kitchen magic. When I began to learn about witchcraft through the lens of Wicca and the Wheel of the Year, I found that my spiritual connection to the kitchen strengthened in a phenomenal way. That meditative state I found while cooking or baking was transformed into a meaningful focus on manifesting and setting intentions through my food. I loved learning about seasonal and symbolic correspondences of ingredients. Moreover, I became enamored with the folklore of food as it relates to magic. Combining all of these ideas and experiences, I began to create recipes that celebrated the idea of "Kitchen Witchcraft."

Reader's Guide

So now that I've introduced the Witch of Whimsy, on the face, I feel that it's time to introduce myself again as the woman behind the witchcraft. I'm Regan Ralston, the author and artist behind this book and behind all the artwork and verse associated with the studio "Water of Whimsy." My most beloved medium to work with is watercolor, hence "Water" of Whimsy. I began my love affair with this art form when I picked up my first paintbrush around age three. My grandmother, Nana, taught me the basics of watercolor and with my early lessons I painted a recreation of the character Ariel from *The Little Mermaid*. Already, my passion for storytelling, folklore and fantasy were blooming. Since then, my craft has been primarily self guided, except for some wonderful art courses at university. I've always fantasized that I could be the village artist, a lone creative who finds satisfaction and fulfillment sharing their works with a small collection of near and dear ones. Imagine my surprise, dear reader, that my little village has grown to include so many more than just neighbors and family.

In this collection of recipes and rituals, you'll find allusions to many of my favorite folktales and fictions. One collection of particular fondness for me is the section on "Hosting a Sleepy Hollow Soirée." These recipes and stories reflect both my adoration for Washington Irving's iconic tale of Americana horror and my love for travel. After an annual ritual of reading *The Legend of Sleepy Hollow* every Halloween, my husband and I finally decided to travel to the town of the legend—Sleepy Hollow, New York, itself. Travel is an exceptional way to connect with the tales of a place, and I always recommend researching local folklore, cryptids and authors associated with your travel destination. While in Sleepy Hollow, the weather was perfectly gloomy and overcast. We frolicked through stone mansions and walked with reverent trepidation through an oil lamp tour of the town's behemoth of a cemetery. All the while,

Meeting the Witch of Whimsy

Irving's words echoed through my mind: "There are certain half-dreaming moods of mind in which we naturally steal away from noise and glare and seek some quiet haunt where we may indulge our reveries and build our air castles undisturbed." With these words, reread as I write, I now consider the way in which kitchen witchcraft allows for "half-dreaming moods," meditative mental states where silence and ritual come together in a way that allows us to indulge in pure reveries. There's something about a blank canvas, be it paper, a new destination or a kitchen full of ingredients, that invokes whimsy.

Through this book, I hope to provide a gentle map to destinations both familiar and unknown, encouraging time in your mind to "build air castles," and practice your deeply intuitive magic. As you craft these recipes, consider the mysticism in each little component. Much of my fascination with kitchen magic revolves around the symbolism and folkloric attributes of each ingredient. While you read and learn about these associations, it is my hope that you'll create your own culinary stories, hopes and dreams. I wanted to pass along these ideas so that every burgeoning Kitchen Witch can grow confidently into that very title: "Kitchen Witch." While you work through the book, morning to night, remember to revel in the transformative magic that resides within your cozy kitchen. The stove is, in many ways, the heart of the home. It is my hope that every recipe and practice will keep you close to this beating heart, where you can feel its drum-like reverberations throughout your everyday life.

A Note on Magic

When I speak of magic, I am speaking of an infinite idea with many connections and corresponding ideals. It was important to me in writing this book that my idea of magic be presented in a way that was both sincere and yet, shifting. I know that, just as within any spiritual practice, the perceptions and practices of individuals may vary widely and drastically. While I don't subscribe to any one particular magical practice, I am influenced by the ideas of Wicca and neo-paganism. In particular, I find magic to be closely related to Wiccan Priest Leo Martello's definition, "superpowers that reside in the natural." As in Wicca, I utilize language to describe this supernatural yet natural force, magic. Moreover, I adopt and proudly utilize the term "Witch" and "witchcraft" in much of my own practice. As you read through this work, I hope I've provided enough nuance and explanatory context to make my writing relevant to your own needs and desires.

Morning

> *"Every morning was a cheerful invitation to make my life of equal simplicity, and I may say innocence, with Nature herself."*
>
> – Henry David Thoreau, *Walden*

Morning mists bring with them an unparalleled bounty of sacred renewal and hope. In many spiritual practices there are rituals associated with the new dawn. In a nunnery, women may rush, with robes swinging, to an early matins. For those who practice yoga, the morning could be greeted with Surya Namaskar, or sun salutations. Just as with these ancient traditions, your faith in a magical life may maintain a similar ebb and flow of ritual, devotion and meditation. So, it is with a fresh heart that we should greet the day, honoring this time with intentional practices for our path ahead.

While there are a million ways to begin your morning, there's one agreed-upon essential from which we all benefit: breakfast. A meal dear to Tolkien's hobbits, breakfast allows for the opportunity to create a spell made from simple ingredients to bless your day and the day of those you may reside with. Your morning enchantments don't require anything fancy or gourmet. Utilizing the homespun wisdom of kitchen witchcraft, you can find ways to concoct a symbolically meaningful meal all in one simple omelet.

With breakfast served and a body fueled for your tasks ahead, it's finally time to consider the most mystical ritual of many mornings: coffee making. As diverse as snowflakes falling into a mountain of vanilla cold foam, coffee recipes are quite literally potions for purposes from energizing to soothing the soul. Just as with breakfast ingredients, the common components of coffee contain their own magical histories and portfolios.

Coffee concoction in hand, where are your thoughts headed? Are you preparing for work? Planning activities with the family? Maybe you're settling in to enjoy some downtime? Our days vary, and some mornings are far from restful. Yet, morning is a time full of new-faced sunlight and singing birds. It is a time when many can harness something quick in their minds, something just awakening. As an artist, I find that these blue hours in my studio, with mourning doves cooing softly, are some of the most untethered from reality. Often alone at that time of day, I enjoy the liminality of newness, utilizing the moments to engage in something rough and creative. It is a practice that I always recommend, and there are many ways to pursue creation during such a whimsical hour. Depending on your own connection to each of these pursuits, consider how you could integrate them into your day as a form of morning meditation and whimsy.

Bullet Journaling

If you find yourself overwhelmed by the strict organization of a normal planner, then bullet journaling might be for you. The idea behind bullet journaling is to put your ideas onto the page in a mishmash of methods, with varying levels of intention and organization. A bullet journal is what you make of it, meaning that it can be a collection of lists, images, paragraphs or other information. In my daily practice, I keep a bullet journal that acts as my daily planner. This way, I loosely collect my thoughts around what is ahead, but I remove the strict structure of a to-do list or calendar. Rather, this is a place for me to consider all that is to come and to enjoy the intention of looking at it all from an unfocused bird's-eye view.

Morning

Free Verse

Free verse is a style of poetry that does not rely on the mechanics of rhyming or other traditional poetic techniques. Rather, free verse poetry can be anything from a stream-of-consciousness collection of words to an intentional and organized piece that closely resembles prose. I find that free verse is a meaningful way of connecting to the subconscious, utilizing a stream-of-consciousness technique to write about any topic from the weather to your current emotional state. I recommend this practice for anyone interested in starting the day with a flex of the imagination as a way to connect to your still-waking mindscape.

Just as early hours are spent on wobbly legs and with slowly collected thoughts, these creative practices should mimic the stretching of morning motions. Extend the muscles of your imagination, flexing phosphorescent wings and unclenching hands made of marshmallow. Let your dreams from the night before flow onto a page, lingering in that place we can only reach outside of our own consciousness. Once you've released all that bright and new magic onto a canvas, you can begin to organize the edges just as you've brought yourself to order through a meaningful meal and meditation, with the extra elixir of that fresh coffee.

Now, I know I've essentially recommended starting your day with breakfast, coffee and some loose planner writing. You might say to yourself, "This isn't magical at all!" To that I will respond simply with my own adage: Magic is what you make of it. In penning these pages, I hope to continue reminding myself and my readers of magic in the everyday. As children, we see so clearly the whimsy all around us. Peter Pan and his pixies are always waiting at the window to whisk us away to Neverland. What if I told you that this magic didn't go away? Our magic has grown inside of us through the years and recognizing mystery in simple moments is key to unleashing the magic that's been with you all along. Now, with open eyes, I can say that magic isn't all about fairy dust and dream worlds, rather it's about celebrating the divine in being alive on this magnificent Earth, day after day.

Morning Meditation

I am open to this day
And the light that shines forth
From a sun just waking,
As I am from dreams
May the light guide my path
As I step into a purpose
Full of intention
And vitality
I know who I am
And I know where I am going
I will take my time
Reaching for the sky
May the earth soften
Where I tread
And may the wind
Guide my way

COFFEE CONCOCTIONS & DAILY AFFIRMATIONS

While we associate coffee with muted tones of brown and tan, the bean itself begins as a bright red berry known as the coffee cherry. Through the process of becoming a beverage we recognize and love, the tiny coffee bean must go through a transfiguration that pushes its flavor and essence to its prime. In this practice, you will harness that transformative power as a conduit to fulfill your own intentions. Through meditation and simple affirmation, your morning cup of coffee can become a portal to fulfilling your daily desires and ridding yourself of negative energies.

As you're making your morning coffee, consider the varying rituals going into that morning cup. Do you grind your own beans? How do you feel when the smell of fresh ground coffee hits your nose? If you feel calm, then consider pairing an affirmation with the practice of grinding coffee. Similarly, if you use a French press, perhaps the act of pressing the coffee fills you with a feeling of empowerment to banish that which isn't serving you. The key to the following exercise should be tailored to your own routines and needs, as artificiality is a negative weight upon meaningful connection to yourself and your desires. If one of these recommendations doesn't feel natural to you, then follow your intuition and mix it up to fit the flow of your own magic. The ritual I am suggesting here includes the practice of stirring a cup of coffee and pairing this physical motion with affirmations as a form of incantation.

The Ritual: Stirring Your Worries Away

A true classic in the lore of witchery, we know there is power in stirring the boiling cauldron. According to folklore and many practitioners, you should stir your coffee in a clockwise direction to invite energies and intentions within yourself. On the other hand, you can stir in a counterclockwise direction to banish or push away stressors and pressures. For example, this morning I was feeling a bit frazzled with my mind going in a million directions. In my interpretation of this ritual, I decided to stir my cup clockwise, to invite in positive intentions, with the following affirmation: "I have the tools to direct my energies today." In forming an affirmation, I want to set a realistic and authentic tone. It would have felt insincere to say "I am successful" as an affirmation because that's not necessarily how I felt or how I needed to meet my needs where they were. You need to believe your affirmation, so be considerate of yourself when planning this simple incantation.

Suggested Affirmations for Inviting the Positive

"I will do my best to focus on what I can control."

"Today I will give myself grace."

"I am open to where my feelings will guide me."

"Today is a gift that I will savor."

Suggested Affirmations for Banishing the Negative

"I will do my best to move past this situation."

"Today I will not give power to what I can't control."

"These struggles will soon pass."

"These feelings are negative, but they won't overcome me."

Finally, one of the most important parts of any spell or ritual is the closing. To finish this practice, I recommend a brief visualization meditation. Stir and repeat the final affirmation, and when you feel it's time to stop stirring, consider the cup full of a bright energy. Let the colors stir as the coffee finishes its wobbling whirlpool. Then, close your eyes and take a sip of the beverage you've poured all this love and intention into. Imagine drinking down the bright light and colors that you've envisioned; think of those intentions spreading throughout your body as the warmth of the beverage hits your chest and rests satisfyingly in your stomach. As you open your eyes, the ritual closes and the day has begun with a meaningful thought exercise in magic and intention.

Ingredients

1 cup (82 g) coffee or espresso beans

2 tbsp (16 g) ground cinnamon

½ tsp ginger

2–3 cloves

½ tsp nutmeg

1 tsp brown sugar, or to taste

1–2 tbsp (15–30 ml) milk, or to taste

Spiced Coffee or Espresso

Coffee is one of those elixirs that most all recognize as a kind of speeding agent. Even now, you may be indulging in the early morning cup to quicken your eyes opening and take in the day. Sometimes, when feeling sluggish, we'll brew that extra pot to help us enliven our pace. Similarly, in magic making, coffee is viewed as a quickening ingredient. According to some folklore, you might add coffee to a dry spell in order to hasten the results of those intentions. In this recipe, we'll be utilizing coffee or espresso to quickly evoke a sense of blissful balance. The primary spice ingredients will be cinnamon, for joy, and clove, for harmony. Supplemental to these focus ingredients are ginger, for increased energy, and nutmeg, for rejuvenation.

To create your own unique quickened spell, consider adding or mixing alternative spices. Almost every spice has its own associated magical correspondence, but most important in magic making is your intention setting. Feel free to get creative, and never underestimate the power of your personal associations. For example, while cinnamon may often be associated with joy, I also associate this spice with a sense of calm. Although that's not a common reading of the ingredient, I feel that in my own spell work, this spice may be used to elicit restfulness.

Serves 12+

Begin by placing the beans, cinnamon, ginger, cloves and nutmeg in a coffee grinder. Grind the mixture until smooth, or until prepared to the right coarseness for your preferred brewing method.

Brew the coffee or espresso mixture with your preferred method. Lastly, add the brown sugar and milk to taste.

Ingredients

1 tsp matcha powder, culinary-grade or ceremonial-grade

2 tsp (10 g) cocoa-mix powder

3 tsp (15 ml) hot water, for mixing

1 cup (240 ml) milk, or milk alternative

Dash of salt

Honey, to taste

Matcha Mocha

In the dark of winter, sometimes our bodies yearn for green. Whether it's sunlight we miss or the warmth and freedom of a summer day, it's certain that a little green helps us feel a lot closer to those golden hours. This recipe combines the dark deliciousness of hot chocolate with the earthy and heartening flavors of matcha. Matcha is a finely ground powder processed from shade-grown tea leaves, traditionally consumed in East Asia. While this tea has a history in spiritual tea ceremonies, the flavor, and the beverage itself, has made its way into the mainstream culinary arts.

This recipe utilizes color to integrate bright earth tones into otherwise darkened hours. I envision this beverage being perfect for long winter days. As you blend the lovely green matcha into soft brown cocoa, envision that green blending into your own dusky day. When you drink this cup of chocolatey umami, remember that the bounty of summer days is always with you.

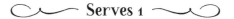 **Serves 1**

Sift the matcha and cocoa mix until smooth, and place the mixture in a small bowl. Then, add the hot water and whisk with a traditional matcha bamboo blender until foamed. If you do not have a bamboo blender, then use a standard whisk. It is best to mix from side to side or up and down, instead of in a circular pattern.

After your matcha-cocoa mix is foamed, place the milk in a saucepan on the stove and heat until steamed, to about 150°F (65°C). Add the steamed milk to your matcha mixture and blend gently. Finally, flavor with a dash of salt and honey to taste.

Ingredients

²⁄₃ cup (160 ml) water

1 Earl Grey tea bag

¼ tsp pansy syrup (page 98)

¼ tsp vanilla

2 tbsp (30 ml) honey

²⁄₃ cup (160 ml) milk, or milk alternative

Dried or fresh pansy flowers, to garnish

Pansy Field Fog

When I think of pansies, the first image that comes to mind is my Nana's cobble-stone raised garden. In the early spring, my sisters and I helped to garden and plant these beds with bright rows of pansies, sweet potato vines and marigolds. The pansies were my favorite because they always seemed to be smiling at me with their vibrantly painted faces.

It follows that in much lore, pansies are regarded as being associated with happiness and love. In this recipe, we'll be utilizing this dainty flower to create the perfect tipple for a literal or proverbial rainy day. With just a drop of pansy syrup, this latte goes from mundane to magical.

Serves 1

Brew the tea to package specifications. Add the syrup, vanilla and honey to your tea mixture and then strain into a cup.

Froth the milk using a milk frother and then pour it slowly into the tea. Spoon the leftover milk froth on the top of the beverage and garnish with pansies.

THE MYSTICAL MAGIC OF
A TEATIME RITUAL

In the morning, tea may be one of the first rituals that you accomplish, perhaps with bleary eyes and a mind just waking. As you select your tea, maybe you first consider flavor or caffeine content. Maybe you're wondering what blend will complement that morning scone. While all these considerations are wonderful, you might also consider the symbolic significance of each tea blend. Are you longing to bring sunlight into a cloudy day? Perhaps you're preparing for a visit from a friend? Each of the teas in this section will provide varied symbolic and magical accents, pairing well with some activities and mindsets over others.

In accompaniment with the morning ritual of tea making, I suggest practicing a little folk magic known as sachet making. The idea of sachet making is that you're combining herbs, flowers and other fragrant or significant pieces to a small bag. This bag, or sachet, is then meant to be carried with you as a sort of totem or spell that will continue to enact its symbolic magic through the day. Alternatively, some sachets are prepared as spells that may be used at night. These sachets would be perhaps hidden under a pillow or left on the nightstand.

The Ritual: A Spell in Your Pocket

While concocting your tea blend, combine the same ingredients into a small sachet. As you drink your finished tea, consider the intentions that went into that particular cup and corresponding sachet. The secret of this ritual is the intentional and physical motions of combining symbolically significant herbs and ingredients in a way that resonates with your given state and desires. While I don't particularly believe any single sachet will automatically enact its given spell, I do believe there is goodness in continual meditation on a particular sentiment or desire.

As you carry your sachet throughout the day, practice asking yourself relevant questions that pertain to that sachet's particular portents. For example, if you're carrying a sunshine tea sachet, ask yourself "Why did I feel that I needed sunlight in my day?" Meditate on these questions and revel in the answers that may arise.

Ingredients

2 bags hibiscus tea

2 cups (480 ml) water

2 cups (480 ml) orange juice

Ice, to serve

Lemon slices, to garnish

Sunshine Tea

When you're longing for the vibrant energy of sunlight, there's no better ingredient to reach for than citrus. Bright and rejuvenating as the sun itself, this recipe features orange juice as a conduit for solar magic. While the citrus will alleviate any cloudy-day haze, the addition of hibiscus provides a different kind of warmth. Hibiscus is most commonly associated with the ideal of love, and when looking at the beautiful bud it's not hard to imagine why. In Tahiti and Hawaii, there's a courting tradition associated with this flower. If a hibiscus is worn behind a woman's left ear, then she is "taken." If a hibiscus is worn behind a woman's right ear, then she is interested in pursuing a relationship.

Marrying the tropical ingredients of citrus and hibiscus, this tea will act as a transportive spell, sailing you to tropical shores where love and light permeate everything down to the smallest crystalline grain of sand.

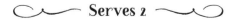

Serves 2

Brew the bags of hibiscus tea in the water. Combine the tea and orange juice in a heat-resistant pitcher and refrigerate until cool. Serve on ice with lemon slices as garnish.

Ingredients

½ tsp lavender leaves

2–3 fresh mint leaves

1 cup (240 ml) water

Sweetened almond milk, to taste

Honey, to taste

Self-Soothing Tea

Some mornings begin with lots of stressors, stemming from worries about the day ahead. When you're feeling the pressure on a morning such as this, it's time to reach for lavender. Combining the relaxing qualities of lavender with the soothing flavors of mint, this tea is perfect for easing nerves and anxieties. While you drink this beverage, also take time to enjoy its delicate aroma, as lavender and mint are both popular ingredients in aromatherapy for relaxation.

When sourcing your lavender and mint leaves, be sure to find culinary grade products. Refrain from collecting your own herbs unless you're confident in their culinary safety.

Serves 1

Place your lavender leaves and mint leaves into a tea bag or tea strainer. Heat the water, and pour it over the blend. Add almond milk to the tea, to taste. Add honey, to sweeten as needed.

Ingredients

2 bags cranberry tea, your preferred brand

2 tsp (2 g) dried rose flowers

2 cups (480 ml) water

2 tbsp (30 ml) honey

Roseberry Tea

This recipe is made for those days where you're feeling burnt out and worn down. With cranberry at the forefront, this elixir is packed full of wholesome vitamins including vitamins C, E and K. With rose as an undertone, the beverage becomes complex and fragrant with a bountiful floral arrangement heightened by bee-sweetened honey.

The magical correspondences of this spell are varied and will depend upon your own intuition's guidance. Cranberry corresponds to the themes of abundance and seasonal festivities, and it is often associated with the time between the autumn equinox and the winter solstice. Cranberry features in so many holiday festivities, surrounding the ideals of family and communion. However, it can also represent love with its vibrant red hue and mysteriously complex flavors. Pairing the cranberry with rose, one might celebrate the love of family or the romantic love of a partner. Whatever the case may be, this is a drink best enjoyed with company!

When sourcing your rose flowers, be sure to select a culinary-grade petal.

Serves 2

Place the tea bags and flower petals in a heat-resistant cup and heat the water to boiling. Pour the boiling water over the tea mixture and let it steep for 2 minutes. Once it is steeped, strain and flavor with the honey.

Ingredients

4 cinnamon sticks

4 cups (960 ml) water

Splash of apple cider vinegar

Lemon juice, to taste

Kitchen Witch's Tea

The Kitchen Witch is resourceful, honoring every ingredient for its many merits and hidden properties. With a deep love for home and the hearth, every spell is edible in its final form. Honing age-old knowledge of the most complex combinations, to the simplest kitchen tricks, this Witch is always ready for guests with a hot cup of Kitchen Witch's Tea.

This tea features one of the most versatile ingredients in kitchen magic: cinnamon. With beautiful simplicity, this beverage is best served warm and to share. Cinnamon is known for its comforting aroma and delicately spiced flavor. Long revered for its scent both cooked and burned as incense, some of the earliest references to this spice are in relation to its use in religious ceremonies. Similarly sacred in Kitchen Witchcraft, it makes sense that this is the Kitchen Witch's chosen brew.

Serves 4

Place the cinnamon sticks and water into a pot with a lid and bring everything to a boil. Cover and simmer for 10 to 15 minutes, tasting for flavor every few minutes (the longer you steep, the stronger the cinnamon taste). Serve warm with a splash of apple cider vinegar and lemon juice, to taste.

PARFAITS TO CELEBRATE THE SEASON

The beauty in a parfait is its interplay between color and texture, featuring loads of fresh fruit and beautifully tangy yogurt. With these recipes in particular, you can make a point to celebrate the season by incorporating the freshest produce and accompanying spices. One of the best forms of kitchen magic, in my opinion, is celebrating what is happening outside. That is, if it's apple season, I want my kitchen to be bursting with fresh local apples. Of course, I live in upstate New York, so apple season is an entire event in and of itself.

While we utilize the freshest and greenest around us, it is also important magically and ethically to consider our impact on the Earth. We're in a reciprocal relationship with our gardens, as they tend us, and we tend them. So too, our relationship with all natural things should flow, as best we can make them. In this ritual, I incorporate the idea of composting into a ritual of gratitude for the earth.

The Ritual: Thanks to the Garden

As you cook throughout the week, it's likely you will accrue a plethora of natural sediment and garbage. If you're able, consider collecting these pieces for compost. Lots of local gardens and shared allotments have a public compost pile, which I highly recommend utilizing when you're able. Even if it's not always possible, this ritual of thanks can be completed as sparsely or frequently as it makes sense for your own life.

Gather the pieces you wish to compost and prepare them for the compost bin. On top of the composted materials, arrange a few pieces of freshly cut vegetables or fruits as a sort of offering to Mother Earth. If you're spiritually connected with a nature-based deity or Genius loci (protective spirit of a place), then feel free to include pieces of produce for them as well. These can be simple slices or intricately cut pieces to represent flowers, the sun or any other icon that is meaningful to you.

As you leave the compost in its appropriate place, consider saying a gentle prayer of thanks. I've included such a gratitude below, and you're more than welcome to share it, if it resonates.

"From the garden you grew and through our plate you nurtured us.

Thank you for your bounty and the energy it provided. May you return and grow once more.

As above, so below."

Ingredients

4 cups (576 g) strawberries

¼ cup (50 g) granulated sugar

10–15 vanilla wafer cookies

1½ cups (360 ml) Greek yogurt

1 cup (240 ml) whipped cream

Strawberry Shortcake Parfait

Strawberries grow with their seeds on the outside of the plant, and they're one of the few fruits that can germinate even when soil is not present. The humble strawberry represents the power of internal preparation and persistence. With this recipe, you can be reminded to start the day with an internal locus of control and strength. Whatever the outside world may bring, you are equipped to move forward, unhindered.

Less metaphorically, this recipe features my favorite flavors of the springy strawberry shortcake dessert. With hearty Greek yogurt and delectable fresh strawberries, this parfait is certain to help your day start on the right garden path.

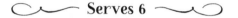

Serves 6

Begin by quartering the strawberries and mixing them with the sugar, then refrigerate for 30 minutes. Meanwhile, chop or grind the wafer cookies until they're lightly crumbed. Assemble the parfait in a parfait glass with a layer of strawberries, cookies and yogurt. Repeat if necessary and top with whipped cream. Garnish with additional strawberry slices and cookie crumbs.

Ingredients

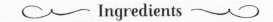

4 medium-sized apples

¼ cup (60 ml) water

½ cup (100 g) granulated sugar

1½ tsp (4 g) cinnamon

¼ tsp nutmeg

3 cups (326 g) granola

4 cups (960 ml) vanilla yogurt

Syrup, for topping

Cinnamon Apple Parfait

In Arthurian legend, Avalon is a location known for its mystical magic and witchcraft. Interestingly enough, Avalon, translated from its original dialect, literally means "isle of [fruit or] apples." Avalon is often said to be home to Arthur's sister, the enchantress, Morgan le Fay. It's not unusual that this Island of Apples is a place of such magic, because apples themselves have long been a part of mystical tales and lore. Whether depicted as a life-giving vessel or a poisonous curse, the apple is a bearer of potent magic.

In witchcraft, the apple is revered for both its many correspondences as well as its symbolic significance. If you slice an apple in half, you'll reveal a pentagram of seeds at its center, representing Earth, air, water and fire, bound by a universal spirit. This fruit is also heavily featured in Samhain celebrations, as it's often depicted as the fruit of the dead and becomes plentiful during the autumn months.

This recipe combines the comforting and nostalgic spice of cinnamon with potent apple magic, to create a parfait befitting any fall morning. When cutting the apples, consider removing a cross section with the pentagram seed star on full display to keep and dry for your altar.

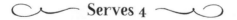

Serves 4

Peel and slice the apples into ½-inch (1-cm) cubes and place them in a saucepan. Add the water, sugar, cinnamon and nutmeg to the pan and bring to a simmer. Let simmer until the apple mixture is syrupy and thickened, about 10 minutes. Remove the mixture from the heat and place it in a bowl, then refrigerate until cooled.

To assemble the parfait, layer the apples, granola and yogurt until the glass is full. Top with additional granola and a drizzle of syrup.

Ingredients

For the Chocolate Granola

½ cup (120 ml) coconut oil

½ cup (120 ml) honey

1 tbsp (15 ml) vanilla extract

½ cup (44 g) cocoa powder

¼ cup (55 g) dark brown sugar

4 cups (360 g) rolled oats

1 tsp salt

¾ cup (126 g) chocolate chips

For the Parfait

2 cups (480 ml) yogurt

½ cup (120 ml) cherry jam

1 cup (163 g) granola

Whipped cream, for topping

Maraschino cherries, for topping

Black Forest Parfait

The Black Forest in Germany is named, legend goes, because the trees are so tall and so thick near the sky that they block out the sun. Everything within the forest walks in darkness, and this forest is also said to have inspired the very tales of the Brothers Grimm, including "Hansel and Gretel" and "Rapunzel." In the culinary world, Black Forest has a more common association: the Black Forest cake!

Featuring chocolatey flavors mixed with the dark sweetness of cherry, this is a recipe to rival even the sweetest breakfast confectionary. This parfait is meant to celebrate decadence, even in the first morning meal. The magic of the cherry is rooted in deep and sensual magic, often associated with aphrodisiacs. As you indulge in this morning meal, revel in the decadence of the unknown. Luxuriate in the spaces where shadows may fall, because from those sources may arise beautiful inspiration.

Serves 2, plus additional chocolate granola

Begin by making the chocolate granola. Preheat the oven to 350°F (175°C). Then, mix together the oil, honey and vanilla until smooth. In a separate bowl, combine the cocoa, brown sugar, oats and salt. Pour the wet mixture over the dry ingredients and blend until evenly coated. Spread the oat mixture onto a baking pan lined with baking paper and bake for 15 minutes. Mix the spread and then bake for a final 10 to 15 minutes. When cool, top with chocolate chips and store in an airtight container.

To assemble the parfait, layer the yogurt, jam and granola in a parfait glass. Repeat until the glass is full, then top with whipped cream and a maraschino cherry.

PRIMING YOUR DAY WITH
BREAKFAST CORRESPONDENCES

As you'll notice in many of my recipe introductions, much of my perspective on magic is inspired by folklore, history and symbolism. There's an interplay between myth and universal truths that fascinates me and keeps me coming back story after story, looking for synchronicities and enlightenment. Something about kitchen magic that lends itself to this kind of thinking is the use of varied ingredients with different flavors and auras that come to the forefront of any given recipe. When I'm working to incorporate something into my life, it's often that I'll refer to my personal grimoire for noted herbal correspondences.

While most ingredients have an entire history and ample folklore to call upon, herbs themselves are unique for the plethora of mythos and beliefs surrounding them. From ancient burial rites to a hedge witch's garden, herbalism is an art unto itself. In this ritual, I encourage a bit of journaling to create your own personal grimoire page surrounding the idea of herbs and their respective symbolisms.

The Ritual:
Building a Grimoire Page for Herbal Magic

A grimoire is a personal diary kept by a Witch or warlock that documents their own spells and magical musings. In this activity, I encourage you to read through the following correspondences in order to journal about your own associations with a handful of common herbs. While the correspondence list is a starting place, personal association is crucial for potent magic. If some of these descriptions don't resonate with you, then move away from those and drift toward personal experience.

- Basil - love, good wishes, wealth
- Bay Leaf - victory, courage and strength
- Cilantro - prosperity and longevity
- Oregano - joy and a ward against negativity
- Parsley - death and rebirth, useful knowledge
- Garlic - protection against evil

Ingredients

Handful of spinach

1 tbsp (15 ml) olive oil, divided

3–4 large eggs, scrambled in a bowl

¼ cup (28 g) Gruyère cheese

3–4 baby potatoes, diced and roasted

½ cup (75 g) cherry tomatoes, diced

Parsley, for topping

Garden Abundance Omelet

Whether picking the ingredients from your own garden or snagging them at the local farmer's market, this recipe features garden staples including cherry tomatoes and spinach. One of my favorite garden plants is the tomato because it thrives and grows so happily almost anywhere. When we had a potted garden on our apartment patio, I celebrated every single little orange, red and yellow gem that sprouted throughout the summer.

According to some folklore, the tomato acts as a shield against negative energies. It is said that if you place a tomato on the windowsill, you can protect against evil spirits, similar to garlic's purported effect against vampires. Combining this red protective fruit with hearty potato and spinach, this omelet is ready to provide you with confidence and shelter against negativity throughout the day.

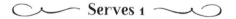

Serves 1

Begin by wilting the spinach. To a skillet, add ½ tablespoon (7.5 ml) of oil and the spinach. Let the spinach cook until just wilted and set aside.

Prepare another small skillet with the remaining ½ tablespoon (7.5 ml) of oil and cook over medium heat. Add the eggs until the bottom of the skillet is covered. While the eggs cook, layer the Gruyère, potatoes, wilted spinach and tomatoes. When the egg begins to pull away from the sides of the pan, fold them over, creating a semicircle. Serve hot with fresh parsley and more tomatoes as garnish.

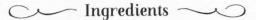

Ingredients

For the Mashed Potatoes
4 potatoes

2 tbsp (28 g) butter

1½ tsp (9 g) salt

¼ cup (60 ml) milk

For the Pancakes
2 cups (600 g) mashed
potatoes

2 eggs

¼ cup (31 g) flour

2–3 tbsp (30–45 ml) milk,
plus more as needed

2 tbsp (6 g) diced, fresh chives

½ tsp garlic powder

¼ tsp paprika

1–2 tbsp (15–30 ml) oil,
for the pan

For Serving
Butter, sour cream or
cream cheese

Potato and Chive Pancakes

In some folk medicine, it was prescribed that patients suffering from arthritis or rheumatism carry a potato in their pocket to help alleviate the aches and pains of everyday life. When I used to feel sick, my mother offered a certain selection of foods for me, and mashed potatoes were always on that menu. Similarly, my husband's mother served him comforting homemade chicken soup on top of steaming mashed potatoes.

While this recipe isn't for carrying in your pocket, it's certainly meant to invoke all of the same heartening and healthful energies of that common potato-pocket lore. In witchcraft, the potato represents stability and the basic necessities of life. As you enjoy these pancakes, take comfort in the everyday blessings that surround you.

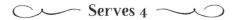

Serves 4

Begin by preparing the mashed potatoes. Peel and quarter the potatoes and then add them to a large pot. Boil the potatoes in water for about 15 to 20 minutes, or until tender. Mash the potatoes and mix in the butter, salt and milk.

To prepare the pancakes, in a large bowl add the mashed potatoes, eggs, flour, milk, chives, garlic powder and paprika. Mix well and add more milk as needed. The batter should be somewhat smooth and easy to pour. Prepare the skillet by heating the oil at medium heat and pour ¼ cup (60 ml) of the batter mixture into the skillet. Brown the pancake for 2 to 3 minutes per side, or until golden brown and crisp on the edges before removing it from the heat to cool.

Serve the pancakes with butter, sour cream or cream cheese.

Ingredients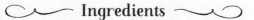

For the Buns

2¼ tsp (10 g) active dry yeast

1 cup (240 ml) whole milk, warm

½ cup (100 g) granulated sugar

⅓ cup (80 ml) melted butter

2 large eggs

1 tsp salt

4 cups (500 g) flour

For the Filling

1 cup (220 g) brown sugar

2 tbsp (16 g) cinnamon

¼ tsp nutmeg

1 cup (117 g) chopped walnuts

½ cup (114 g) unsalted butter, softened

For the Icing

3 cups (360 g) powdered sugar

½ cup (120 ml) butter, melted

2 tsp (10 ml) vanilla extract

2 tbsp (30 ml) whole milk

Stuffed Cinnamon Buns

It's said that you can make a wish with a walnut if you know the way. First, you remove the walnut from the shell, and as you eat its rich meat, you think of a wish. Then, you write that wish down and seal it within the walnut's shell. You can carry this wish with you, hang it in the home or keep it under your pillow until the wish comes true.

In this recipe, we're utilizing a similar hiding magic with walnuts as the conduits. While you craft this recipe, consider a wish that you have in your heart. When you sprinkle the walnuts over your dough, whisper a wish to yourself, or speak it in your mind. As you roll up the dough, imagine the sealing of a walnut shell, with all its potent, fulfilling magic. These delectable buns are now sweetened with your dreams and dappled with cinnamon, an ingredient known in witchcraft as a drawing energy.

When sharing these buns with family or friends, you can share in the wish magic by encouraging them to consider their own sweetest wishes!

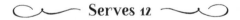 Serves 12

First, make the buns. Dissolve the yeast in your warmed milk for 5 to 10 minutes, or until the mixture begins to bubble. Then in another bowl, combine the yeast mixture, granulated sugar, butter, eggs and salt. Mix until blended, then add the flour in gradually until a sticky dough has formed. Turn out the dough onto a floured surface and knead until smooth, about 5 to 10 minutes. Transfer your dough to a greased bowl, then cover and move it to a warm spot. Let the dough rise for an hour, or until doubled in size.

While the dough rises, prepare the filling. Combine the brown sugar, cinnamon and nutmeg. Grind the walnuts until they are approximately pea sized.

(continued)

Punch down the dough and then roll it out on a flat surface until the dough has formed a rectangle, about 9 x 13 inches (23 x 33 cm). Cover the dough in a layer of butter and then add the cinnamon sugar mixture sprinkled on top. Finally, add the walnuts on top of the sugar mixture. Roll the dough into itself, starting from the longest side of the rectangle (like a jelly roll). Once the dough is rolled, cut crosswise into about sixteen individual buns. Place the buns into a 9 x 13–inch (23 x 33 cm) baking dish, cover with a towel, then move to a warm spot. Let the buns rise for an hour, or until they have doubled in size.

While you wait for the buns to rise, prepare the icing. Add the powdered sugar, butter, vanilla and whole milk to a bowl and blend until smooth and creamy. After you've finished making the icing, set the oven to 350°F (175°C).

Once the buns have risen, bake them for 20 to 25 minutes or until golden brown, and top them with icing while they're still warm from the oven.

Noon

"It is the still, yellow kind of afternoon when one is apt to get stuck in a dream if one sits very quiet."

– Dodie Smith

Afternoon magic is a creature harder to capture than most. As it bounds between meetings and events, plans and deadlines block your way while you hurry after those telltale paw prints signaling something more, something mystical. As I write this, outside the window, two spiders weave away industriously at their webs. A squirrel scurries by, no doubt hunting for nuts to store for its winter hoard. The clock is just about to strike the noon hour, and I wait anxiously to hear the bells that will toll from a tower in my little community. This is such a time full of motion and meaning. From the smallest to the largest of us, we feel the call to fill these hours with something, with purpose, with accomplishments under our belt. There's something primordial about the urge to move, to make, to do, and it strikes us hardest at this time of the day when things just seem to happen. Yet, between all of this action, we are subject to the will of our bodies. We need breaks to rest, to eat, to fuel our onward motion. In these moments, we can hone and honor ourselves with a little kitchen magic.

The ritual of teatime is one of those special celebrations that are meant to grace the everyday. Whether sneaking a cuppa in the break room or indulging in a full spread with friends, this magic-full beverage is a potion ready to be catered to your every need and desire. Whether searching for a little bit of energy, or looking to reground with earthy magic, this beverage bolsters a plethora of spells through intention.

Teatime, as we know it in English tradition, became standardized around the nineteenth century in Victorian England. The process of serving tea was highly ritualized, in part because the beverage and its accoutrements were expensively imported from China, where the tradition was strongly rooted. Teatime was already full of such meaning that even aristocratic women would serve their own tea as a symbolic representation of their nurturing effect on the home as a whole.

The timing of what we now view as afternoon tea was similarly solidified around the turn of the nineteenth century. Initially, tea was served as an after-dinner beverage, thought to help digestion. However, in the late 1700s to early 1800s, aristocracy began to serve dinner later and later in the evening. Eventually, it became common for ladies to serve afternoon tea services as a way to hold over their appetites until a late evening dinner. This tradition spread throughout all classes and social statuses but maintained its ideals of luxury and social significance.

Today, teatime has become a well-known ritual full of nostalgia for its legendary beginnings in the cozy halls of coterie. In this section, I'll highlight two special tea services with themes full of summer magic and garden beauty. Each of these tea services feature a selection of treats and confectionery meant to be served with the same nurturing style of old.

Afternoon Meditation

The sun is high in the sky
And I am full of Earth's greenness
As I set to work
Doing the best that I can
May I bless this day with kindness
To share and to receive
May I grace myself with understanding
And compassion
Just as bees buzz
To a hive
So too let me be filled
With instinct and drive
May what is done today
Be done well
And what is left unfinished
Be unburdened

PLANNING A COTTAGE WITCH'S PICNIC

For one of my illustration series, I focused on the different paths of witchcraft practiced both contemporarily and historically. Utilizing common themes and ideals, I organized these groups into different typographies. For example, a Kitchen Witch may utilize baking and cooking as their main preference for magic making. Alternatively, a Sea Witch might find herself drawn to the ocean, utilizing seawater and shells for building spells and quelling storms. In terms of Witch type, the classifications are endless because the paths of witchcraft are many. This is simply a form of organizing and identifying features amongst common practices and beliefs. While working on my illustration series, I covered over twelve types of witches, and still, there were many more suggested by modern magic makers.

The Cottage Witch derives their name from the cozy air they inhabit. Practicing green, kitchen and a variety of other magics, this Witch combines their skills to design the perfect home. Enamored with all things domestic and crafty, they are known to repurpose unusual items into masterful works of art. Enhancing their practice is a skill with flowers and herbs; often, the Cottage Witch tends a beloved garden that keeps the lucky inhabitants of their home cared for. In this section, I create a picnic tailored to the Cottage Witch, featuring lots of garden-fresh flowers and whimsical bounty.

As befits a Cottage Witch, the ritual associated with this section involves the loving scavenging and rehoming of beautiful dishware. Recycling and upcycling as magic is certainly a unique practice, but for a Cottage Witch this is part and parcel of their own particular brand of spell making.

The Ritual: Upcycling Dishware

To prepare for this picnic, you'll need a few small mason-jar style glasses for the Raspberry Cream Pie in a Jar and a handful of coupe-style glasses for the Green Apples and Pansy Syrup. One of the most magical ways to retrieve these items is through upcycling! I find that there's something so whimsical about entering an antique or reuse shop, and I frequent ours anytime I need something with a little vintage flair. Not only do these kinds of stores carry unique and memorable items, but they also help to recycle items that still have lots of life in them.

As you search for the perfect dishware, consider your guests and their unique personalities. Not all of the dishware has to match; let your intuition guide you to find styles that will suit each of your friends or family. If you're unable to shop for your dishware, then consider reusing glasses that naturally make their way into your home; sometimes my jelly comes in a beautiful jar, which would be perfect for reusing!

Once you have your dishware, it's time to start the main focus of this ritual, which is cleansing the glasses and beautifying them for their purpose. Wash the glasses in hot water and soap, making sure to remove any price stickers or stains. If you're working with silver, be sure that it's food safe and treated appropriately. While you're washing, envision the picnic with your friends surrounding you. Let these serene ideals and happy thoughts soak through your hands into the glassware.

Finally, consider adding bows or accents to the glasses in preparation for the picnic. One cute idea, which honors your friends and utilizes crafting magic, would be to tie bows around the pie glasses with little cards attached holding a special note for each individual guest.

Ingredients

For the Salad

5 cups (100 g) mixed greens

½ cup (34 g) dandelion greens

¼ cup (11 g) pansies

¼ cup (11 g) nasturtium flowers

For the Dressing

1 small clove garlic

1 tbsp (15 ml) fresh lemon juice

¼ tsp lemon zest

2–3 tbsp (30–45 ml) extra virgin olive oil

1 tsp salt

¼ tsp ground black pepper, or to taste

Wildflower Salad

Oftentimes, the nasturtium flower is used to represent conquest or victory in war. Perhaps this association arose from the flower's vibrant reds and oranges or its shape, which resembles a shield. Symbolically, this flower represents optimism and accomplishment. As a star of this recipe, the nasturtium flowers are meant to invoke a sense of success, which will follow through the rest of a blessed picnic meal. As you serve subsequent dishes following this salad, remember that the event has been set upon a special red and orange blessing for victory.

Also featured in this recipe are the pansy and the dandelion, two flowers which are found all over wildflower fields in the summertime. While these each have their own special correspondences, the main idea of the recipe is wildflowers. Wild- flowers grow unruly and unbidden, urged on by the spirits of a place to decorate their hidden bowers. Similarly, this salad celebrates and honors local Earth magic in all its bounty.

When sourcing flowers for this recipe, it is important to only purchase culinary-grade product. Do not attempt to harvest these flowers yourself unless you're certain that the flower has not been treated with any chemicals or pesticides. Before incorporating the flowers into your recipe, gently rinse them with water and lay them out to dry on paper towels.

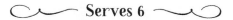

Serves 6

In a large bowl, combine the mixed greens and dandelion greens. Then, arrange the flowers atop the salad in a decorative display.

To create the dressing, begin by dicing the garlic. Combine the garlic, lemon juice and zest in a small bowl and mix. Add the olive oil to the garlic mixture, then the salt and pepper. Note: The nasturtium flowers have a peppery flavor, so keep this in consideration when adding pepper.

Finally, dress the salads on individual serving plates, to each person's taste.

Ingredients

1 cup (232 g) cream cheese

1½ tsp (5 g) poppy seeds

½ tsp lemon juice

⅛ tsp ground black pepper

1 cucumber

12 slices honey wheat sandwich bread, frozen

Poppyseed Tea Sandwiches

In Greek mythology, the poppy is Demeter's emblem, representing life-giving abundance and earthly blessings. Historically found near important agricultural crops such as wheat, the poppy was viewed as deeply intertwined with the nourishment of soil and the cycle of regeneration—life, birth and death. In this recipe, poppy acts as an ode to Demeter's gifts, accenting the bright flavor of garden-grown cucumber and ripe lemon.

At this picnic, associated so deeply with growing things and summer bounty, consider setting aside a plate for the goddess Demeter. This little act represents gratitude for the blessings of agriculture and the fresh nourishment provided by the meal.

Serves 18

In a bowl, combine the cream cheese, poppy seeds, lemon juice and black pepper. Mix until smooth. Then chop the cucumber into fine slices.

To form the sandwiches, spread the cream cheese onto six slices of bread, then add a layer of cucumber slices. Place the remaining six slices of bread on top and cut into 1½-inch (3¾-cm) square sandwiches.

Keep the sandwiches in the fridge, covered with a damp cloth, until ready to thaw and serve to maintain freshness.

Ingredients

2 cups (400 g) granulated sugar

1 cup (45 g) fresh black or purple pansy flowers,
plus more for garnish/topping

1 cup (240 ml) water

6 medium green apples, sliced

Green Apples and Pansy Syrup

According to some folklore, you can ensure and nurture fidelity by splitting an apple with a lover. You eat one half, and your lover eats the other, increasing sincerity and loyalty. In this recipe, the age–old folklore is modified to emphasize friendship and general happiness in platonic relationships. Since you will slice the apple in this recipe, you can easily share it with many people who are dear to you.

Strengthening this little spell is the inclusion of sweetened pansy in the form of pansy syrup. Pansies, with their happy faces and beautiful hues, represent love and friendship. Emphasizing the intentions of the shared apple ritual, this little treat is the edible equivalent of a colorful friendship bracelet.

When sourcing your pansies, be sure to select a culinary grade petal. Be careful harvesting these on your own, unless you're certain of their food safety.

Serves 6

In a food processor, combine the sugar and pansies (saving a handful of pansies for garnish). Process the sugar and pansy mixture for about thirty seconds. Then, add the sugar mixture and water to a saucepan. Bring the mixture to a boil, then reduce and simmer it until the liquid becomes syrup (or coats the back of a spoon), about 10 minutes.

Allow the syrup to cool and serve drizzled over apple slices. Garnish with fresh pansy flowers.

Ingredients

1½ cups (185 g) raspberries,
plus more for topping

½ cup (100 g) granulated sugar

½ cup (120 ml) water

1 cup (232 g) cream cheese

1 tsp vanilla extract

6–8 graham crackers, crushed

16 oz (453 g) whipped cream

Raspberry Cream Pie in a Jar

Raspberry derives its name from the Germanic raspoie, *meaning thicket. This fruit grows within a woody cage of briars and thorns, making it difficult to harvest for even the most determined of foragers. Raspberry only offers its fruits to those who search with gentle and caring hands, teaching us to work our magic similarly.*

As you prepare this dessert, remember the power of your own intentions and emotions. Work with careful cunning so as not to burden the dish with prickly thoughts or residual energies. Set your mind to fill this raspberry delight with warmth and beautiful evocations. When sharing amongst friends, they'll be grateful for all the love and care that went into this dish, from picking prickly bushes to blending sweet intentions.

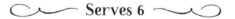 **Serves 6**

In a saucepan, combine the raspberries, sugar and water. Heat on high until simmering, then lower the heat to medium, and let the syrup cook until thickened, about 10 to 15 minutes. Remove the syrup from the heat, strain and set it aside to cool.

In a bowl, combine the cream cheese, vanilla and raspberry syrup. Whip until fluffy and well blended.

To assemble the jars, layer the crushed graham crackers, raspberry filling and whipped cream. Top with extra raspberries and graham cracker crumbs.

Garden Magic Tea Party

"Sometimes since I've been in the garden I've looked up through the trees at the sky and I have had a strange feeling of being happy as if something was pushing and drawing in my chest and making me breathe fast. Magic is always pushing and drawing and making things out of nothing. Everything is made out of magic, leaves and trees, flowers and birds, badgers and foxes and squirrels and people. So it must be all around us. In this garden—in all the places."

– Frances Hodgson Burnett, *The Secret Garden*

This quote is spoken by the protagonist Mary in *The Secret Garden*, one of my favorite books from childhood. I love the way she envisions her breath, in and out, beating almost like the wings of a mystical robin who sings songs and tells of hidden keys. Just as in this fantastical book, so too, our own gardens may teach us about the push and pull of earthly magic. Representing both growth and decay, the garden is full of duality. Success and failure, beauty and plainness are all thriving within the borders of some raised garden bed.

In this ritual, I encourage you to meditate within the liminality of a garden space. Just as Mary found her heart beating, full of magic-making meaning in her garden, so too, may these feelings and experiences open up to you.

The Ritual: Garden Meditation

For this meditation, I recommend that you find a garden or growing space where you can comfortably sit or recline. If you don't have a garden of your own, consider visiting a shared garden space or public garden. Some readers might be lucky enough to have professional botanical gardens near them where they can fully immerse themselves in the realm of growing things.

Once in the garden, sit down upon the earth with your legs crossed and hands flat on the dirt. It's important to connect with all that is around you, to sense and feel for that breathing of magic connecting all things. As you sit, slowly begin to separate your thoughts from everything but the earth below and the sky above. If there's a gentle breeze, breathe in time to the wind and the sound of the leaves as they rustle.

Meditate in this way for as long as you feel comfortable, becoming another growing thing within the garden itself. As you feel your consciousness rising to the surface once more, slowly flutter your eyes open and take in the green around you. Consider all that the garden provides and whisper a quiet thank-you, as you may.

Slowly, come out of your meditation and spend a few more minutes enjoying the garden from your vantage point. Take note of all the living things that thrive, from the squirrels to the seedlings. If you have a particular closing that you like to practice with meditations, then complete that also as you're ready.

For me, I like to close with a simple "as above, so below." State this in your mind or verbalize it before you stand and continue your day.

Ingredients

8 cups (2 L) water

4 rooibos tea bags

1 lemon, juiced

Honey, to taste

Rooibos Iced Tea

Rooibos tea is derived from the plant family Fabaceae, which is grown predominately in South Africa. With a hearty flavor and earthy tones, this tea is perfect for pairing with a garden-themed tea party. Not only is the taste aligned with nature's bounty, but the color of this beverage also takes on an earthy red hue. Sometimes this tea is referred to as bush tea, red tea or red bush tea.

As you indulge in this simple and powerful drink, consider the way in which all the leaves around us provide sustenance and life. Whether drinking their elixir, or breathing clean air, there's much to be thankful for under a bower of bounty.

Serves 8

Boil the water and immerse the rooibos tea bags for steeping, according to package directions. Once the tea is brewed, move it to a pitcher and let it cool in the refrigerator for at least an hour.

To serve, add the lemon juice to the pitcher and then pour the tea over ice in tall glasses. Add honey to taste.

Ingredients

2 cups (250 g) flour

2 tsp (12 g) salt

1 tbsp (14 g) baking powder

⅓ cup (75 g) unsalted butter, cubed

¾ cup (180 ml) heavy whipping cream,
plus more for brushing

1 egg

1 cup (113 g) sharp cheddar cheese, grated

⅓ cup (16 g) fresh chives or scallions, diced

Peter Rabbit's Scone

Peter Rabbit has been creating mischief for over a hundred years through tales of garden grazing and forest frolicking. In honor of his adventures into many a vegetable patch, I've concocted this scone, featuring the fresh green flavors of chive paired with sharp cheddar cheese.

According to some folklore, chive is associated with the ideals of protection. Perhaps this scone would do well for Peter as he attempts to ward off the curmudgeonly Mr. McGregor. While you enjoy this recipe, imagine the fresh garden energies surrounding you in the cozy protection of picket fences and comforting pumpkin vines.

Serves 8

In a bowl, combine the flour, salt and baking powder. Blend this mixture, then add the cubed butter. Continue to blend until the mixture has reached a crumbly consistency.

In a separate bowl, combine the whipping cream and egg. Then, slowly add the wet mixture to your flour mixture and stir. When the dough has reached a dough-like consistency, fold in the cheese and scallions.

Place the mixture on a flat surface and knead it into a ball, then flatten the ball into a disk about 6 inches (15 cm) in diameter. Cut the disk into eight separate triangle pieces and place these on a tray with parchment paper. Place the tray in the freezer for 5 to 10 minutes, until the slices have hardened. While the tray is in the freezer, set your oven to 400°F (200°C).

Lightly brush the scones with heavy whipping cream and bake for about 20 minutes, or until the scones are a light brown color.

Ingredients

¾ cup (168 g) softened butter

2 tbsp (8 g) fresh parsley

2 tbsp (4 g) fresh basil

8 slices of pumpernickel bread

8 stalks of asparagus

2 tsp (10 ml) olive oil

Lemon juice, to taste

Asparagus Sandwiches

In ancient Greece, asparagus was associated with fertility and the goddess of love, Aphrodite. While asparagus may not seem like the most romantic food, it carries associations with affection and fidelity due to this history. Paired with basil, which is said to invoke luck in love, this sandwich is perfect for welcoming happiness into your relationships, romantic or otherwise.

During Tudor times, small pots of basil were given to guests as parting gifts. Consider packaging some of the leftover basil for your party goers to bring home into their own kitchens; these bundles will act like a traveling spell sending your love and well wishes.

 **Serves 8**

Mix the softened butter with the parsley and basil until well blended. Spread the butter mixture onto a piece of pumpernickel bread, then top with a second slice of bread, and cut the sandwich into four squares. Top the sandwiches with asparagus, cut to the width of the sandwiches, and drizzle them with olive oil and lemon juice.

Ingredients

¾ cup (180 ml) water

¾ cup (150 g) granulated sugar

2 tsp (10 ml) rose extract

4 egg whites

Red food coloring, optional

Rose Meringue

One of my favorite myths about the rose flower derives from Hinduism. It is said that Lakshmi, the goddess of wealth and good fortune, was created from 108 large rose petals and 1,008 small rose petals. This lore is particularly poignant to me because my husband and I share the magic number of 108, associating it with our relationship in many ways. For example, when we first met, his home was 108 miles (174 km) away from mine. After five years of marriage, we still love to point out the synchronicities of this number when it appears in our life.

Channeling the magic of Lakshmi's rose petals, this recipe offers abundance through simplicity. The rose-shaped meringue, provides the perfect addition to any tea setting. As you indulge in these confectionaries, consider sending up a message of thanks for the abundance at your table and blessings in your life. If you're feeling extra aligned with Lakshmi and this story, consider finding a way to incorporate the number magic of 108 into your table setting or tea service.

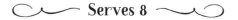

Serves 8

In a saucepan, bring the water, sugar and rose extract to a boil. Simmer for 5 to 10 minutes, until slightly thickened. Set the syrup aside and allow it to cool slightly.

Whip the egg whites in a mixer or with a hand mixer until stiff peaks have formed. Slowly pour the syrup mixture into the whipped egg whites while turning the mixer to beat on high. Pour the syrup in increments, making sure that the whipped eggs do not deflate. It's best if the syrup mixture is added as a light trickle while the mixer churns. Continue to mix and pour until fully combined; the meringue should have a glossy texture. As the meringue finishes, add in a few red food coloring drops, if wanted.

Preheat the oven to 250°F (121°C) and pipe rosettes of the meringue mixture onto a baking sheet. Bake the meringues for one hour, or until hardened. Allow the rosettes to fully cool in the oven before removing and serving.

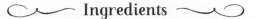

Ingredients

For the Cupcakes
2 large eggs

1 cup (200 g) granulated sugar

1 stick (8 tbsp) (112 g) butter, softened

1 tsp vanilla extract

2 tbsp (30 ml) blood orange juice

1 tsp blood orange zest

2 tsp (3 g) cardamom

1½ cups (188 g) flour

1½ tsp (7 g) baking powder

Pinch of salt

½ cup (120 ml) milk

For the Icing
½ cup (114 g) unsalted butter, softened

2 cups (240 g) powdered sugar

1 tsp vanilla extract

2 tbsp (30 ml) milk

3 drops orange food coloring

Garden Gold Cupcake

The use of cardamom dates back almost 4,000 years to the Egyptians. It featured heavily as a spice associated with both the rituals of life and death. In this recipe, cardamom acts as a heady grounding agent, reminding us of each flower's roots—digging deep into the dark earth and thriving amongst fallen leaves and the residue of decay. For every blooming flower, there is a system of darkness and dirt. As above, so below.

Complementing the spicier notes of cardamom is blood orange. Its visceral color and name remind us of vitality. The combination of all these elements results in a flower that is meant to remind us of the preciousness in life.

Serves 8

Preheat the oven to 350°F (175°C). In a bowl mix together the eggs and granulated sugar until smooth, then add the butter and vanilla. Mix until creamy, then add the orange juice, zest and cardamom. Mix until fully combined.

In a small bowl combine the flour, baking powder and salt. Alternating with the milk, slowly add the dry ingredients to your butter and sugar mixture. Mix until all are combined, being careful not to overmix.

Pour the batter into cupcake molds lined with foil tins, filling each one two-thirds full. Bake the cupcakes for 18 to 20 minutes, or until done. While the cupcakes bake, prepare your icing.

To make the icing, begin by beating the butter until fluffy. Add the powdered sugar, vanilla and milk, whisking as you go to maintain the texture. Finally, add the orange food coloring until the icing has a color similar to a marigold flower.

Once the cupcakes have come out of the oven, cool them to room temperature before icing. With a pipette, cover the cupcakes in a marigold pattern, starting with small splotches of icing in a circular pattern at the center of the cupcake. Branch out with subsequently larger circles of petals until the cupcake is fully covered with icing.

HERBALISM IN LEMONADE LIBATIONS

Lemonade has an inextricable association with sunlight and summertime. From its refreshing taste to vibrant coloring, this beverage is intertwined with solar energies. In this section, I share a variety of lemonade recipes that each add their own whimsical twist to the standard. When I think about drinking lemonade, I imagine sitting in the sunshine somewhere bright and green, with a blue sky overhead. Even in the dead of winter—or especially in the dead of winter—lemonade can bring a boost of sun to my otherwise gray world.

In this ritual, we pair lemonade with the practice of gentle meditation to soak up light energy and rejuvenate our spirit. This ritual can be done anytime you feel that you need a connection with bright, rising energy or solar comfort.

The Ritual: Sunlight Bathing

First, find a source of sunlight and set yourself comfortably within the sun's rays. If it's gray and cloudy, try your best to find a window that lets in some form of natural light. Alternatively, if you're in possession of a light therapy lamp, then this can be used as a substitute for natural lighting.

Once you're settled, take a drink of your lemonade, and let it dance on the tongue. Consider the citrus in its originating grove somewhere hot and scented by blossoms. Imagine the sun's rays dancing amongst the leaves, creating shadow and shade within the fruity bower.

Close your eyes and feel the warmth of the sun permeate your lids, turning everything orange and hazy.

As you fall into a delicate meditation, consider the following mantra: "I am full of light."

After you have sat for a time, slowly open your eyes and gently bring your body back to awareness, moving to become comfortable. Enjoy the rest of your lemonade, envisioning all the light energy inside yourself.

Ingredients

1 handful of freshly picked lavender flowers *or*
1 tsp dried lavender flowers

1 cup (200 g) sugar

2 cups (480 ml) boiling water

8 large lemons

Ice, as desired

Water, to taste

Lavender Lemonade

In ancient Greece, lavender was known as Spikenard, *named after the Syrian city Naarda. In English, the word is derived from the Latin word* lavare, *meaning to wash. This translation follows along the tradition of lavender usage in cleansing both body and spirit. While making the recipe, combining lavender and the vibrant refreshment of homemade lemonade, consider what you wish to wash away. With each sip of this light and refreshing elixir, envision your worries floating beyond, as breezes of lavender surround you with calm.*

When selecting your lavender for this recipe, be sure to use one of the varieties preferred for cooking, such as English Lavender. Remember that less is more when it comes to this ingredient, so be sure to adjust the recipe with caution. After brewing, there may be leftover lavender simple syrup, so be sure to save this for later purposes like flavoring tea or baked goods. If kept in the refrigerator, simple syrup may last up to two weeks.

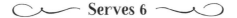

Serves 6

Begin by creating a lavender simple syrup. First, take your lavender flowers and place them in a heat-resistant bowl. Cover the flowers with the sugar and stir by hand until they are covered. Pour the boiling water over the flower and sugar mixture. Stir this concoction until all the sugar is dissolved, then cover and store for 2 to 3 hours, as time allows. Once the mixture has set, strain it, then set it aside.

To create your lemonade base, begin by juicing the lemons. It is helpful to roll the lemons around with your hand on a hard countertop to loosen the juices before juicing. Once you've collected your juice, set it aside.

Finally, prepare your pitcher with ice. Add the lemon juice and water, then mix. Finally, add your simple syrup, to taste.

Serve with a lemon slice and a lavender sprig.

Ingredients

For the Simple Syrup

1 cup (240 ml) water

1 cup (200 g) sugar

For the Lemonade

5–6 lemons

2–3 cups (480–720 ml) cold water

½ cup (46 g) fresh mint leaves

Mint Lemonade

Pliny the Elder, a naturalist and philosopher, documents the uses of mint in ancient Roman culture. Whether worn as a headdress or flavoring a sauce, the herb was revered for its potent flavor and remedying magic. Pliny even goes so far as to suggest the use of mint in drink as an elixir for aiding in the healing of scorpion stings and snake bites.

While we now prefer antivenom and modern solutions to such problems, it's fascinating to think that mint has maintained such a significant role in the culinary and medical arts throughout history. At the root of this lore is an awareness that mint possesses cooling qualities and aroma. This recipe combines the simple flavors of lemon and common mint to provide a mouthful of ancient flavors that soothe the body and mind.

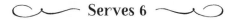

Serves 6

Begin by creating a simple syrup. Combine the water and sugar in a saucepan and bring it to a boil, then reduce the heat to medium and simmer until thickened (about 5 to 10 minutes). Set aside.

Squeeze the lemons until you have about 1 cup (240 ml) of lemon juice. Combine the lemon juice and simple syrup in a pitcher. Add the cold water and mint leaves until the pitcher is full, or to taste.

Refrigerate for 1 hour before serving to allow the mint to fully flavor the beverage.

Ingredients

For the Simple Syrup

1 cup (200 g) sugar

1 cup (240 ml) water

2 cups (246 g) blackberries,
plus more for garnish

For the Lemonade

5–6 lemons

3–6 cups (720 ml–1.5 L)
sparkling water

Sparkling Blackberry Lemonade

One of the most poignant characteristics of blackberry is its vibrant hue. Indulging in fresh blackberries is a decadent experience, incomplete without stained fingers and tongues dyed the color of pansy purple. Historically, blackberry has been used to dye clothing and even hair. With its lovely violet hues, there is certainly color magic in this fruit.

Combining blackberry and beautiful bubbles, this beverage looks like a potion made by fae folk, or fairies. In fact, in folklore, blackberries are sometimes even referred to as "fae fruit." Certainly, this blackberry concoction is perfect for some cottage-side picnic amongst the fair folk themselves.

Serves 6

First, make the simple syrup. In a saucepan combine the sugar, water and blackberries. Bring to a boil and simmer for 10 to 12 minutes, until thickened. While simmering, mash the berries with a potato masher. Lastly, strain the mixture and set it aside.

Squeeze the lemons until you have about 1 cup (240 ml) of lemon juice. Combine the lemon juice and simple syrup in a pitcher. Add sparkling water (to taste) and serve immediately over ice. Garnish with fresh blackberries.

Evening

Twilight reaches us with a gentle embrace, urging creatures back to their dens and bustling the sky toward its final colors. Evening holds the sacred hours when we come together with family and friends to share the adventures of our day. We turn the porch lights on and beckon all to gather at home, around the stove, where warm meals settle onto set tables and hungry hands are washed before a blessing, and the forks and knives begin their dance. In the evening, it's obvious to see magic around the dinner table, with a hearth blazing and candles set. Even on our most harried of nights, there's whimsy in reconnecting with our home and the comforts within.

For me, evening begins with the preparation of dinner. I close out of all my work for the day, stepping away from the studio and shutting the door with a breath of relief. It's just so pleasant to know your work is done, and it's time to settle into those primordial motions of gathering the food around a fire. In many families, everyone comes home at the end of the day. For me, my husband arrives, and it's like a gift each time. We are creatures of community, and evening is that sacred time when our closest companions come back to us. There's something exceptionally magical about cooking for friends and family as they return to you from the great wide world.

In all cultures around the world, mealtime is full of rituals both intricate and simple. In living a magical life, I've come to cement certain rituals which help me to imbue every dinner with whimsy and love. One ritual, which spans across many customs, is the simple inclusion of a blessing. Before you take your first bite of food, consider offering up a prayer, meditation or sentiment of thanks. In this simple act, you will invoke a sense of gratitude that carries with it the ideals of peace and contentment. Another ritual I recommend is eating with others. While this may not seem like a formal ritual, gathering together with the purpose of sharing a meal is ritual enough when you combine it with intention. Conversation over the dinner table is a special time when we're sharing ourselves in our humanity or eating together to sustain our bodies. In this section, I provide a selection of meals meant to be shared with those you cherish. As you prepare each recipe, remember that your intentions and emotions soak into the essence of what you're creating. Cooking is as good as spell work, so be certain to approach your meal making with positive intentions and love.

Evening Meditation

As evening tide washes
The sun from the sky
May I too retire
From my daily labors

I am full of gratitude
For the day behind me
And I am full of joy
For the day yet ahead

May our table be set
With Earth's bounty
And may it sustain us
Through to a new day

I am at peace
With the growing dark
And I will be soothed
By the coming stars

SALAD MAKING WITH
THE GREEN WITCH

Green Magic, as a simple definition, is a form of witchcraft that focuses on crafting spells and rituals through naturally sourced magic found in green spaces, such as forests, gardens and fields. In this section, we're utilizing loads of greens to create delicious and whimsical salads packed with lots of nutrients and flavor. In a way, salad making is its own form of green magic, as it combines different plants to develop the right flavor or purpose in a recipe.

In folklore across the world, green features as a symbolically powerful color. It's associated with gods and goddesses across multiple pantheons in Egyptian, Slavic and Greek mythology. As a way of connecting even more symbolic meaning with the color green, this activity involves a closer look at these green deities and their alignments.

The Ritual: Grimoire Pages—Green Gods & Goddesses

Just as in a previous ritual, this activity calls for you to consider creating your own grimoire page, featuring the following information. A grimoire is a book of spells or a book of knowledge, similar to a personal diary for witches. Your grimoire can be whatever you desire, from personal thoughts to studious notes. The grimoire is meant to act as a quick reference guide for when you're hoping to create a particular spell, or when you're searching for that slippery bit of folklore. The information that I'll share here pertains to Green Magic and associated deities. You might caption this page in your grimoire as such, and feel free to add your own research or associations to those I've included.

Once you're done journaling, it's time to get to salad making, remembering all the mysticism and lore associated with this fantastic color!

Green in Egyptian Mythology

In ancient Egyptian, the word for the green stone malachite meant *joy*. Green represented new life and vegetation flowing from the Nile. However, green was also associated with the God of Death, Osiris, who is often depicted as having green skin. Just as real vegetation, the Egyptians viewed green as a kind of cyclical color— what lives must also die.

Green in Slavic Mythology

In pagan Slavic folklore, there's an entity known as rusalka, which is similar in some ways to a mermaid. According to folklorist Vladimir Propp, rusalka emerge from the water in the spring to provide life-granting moisture to the Earth and fields. They're often depicted with green skin and green hair, thus connecting them with the cyclical green of vegetation and fertility.

Green in Greek Mythology

In ancient Greece, green was associated with Demeter, the daughter of Rhea and Kronos. Demeter is a goddess who presides over the crops, grain, agriculture and fertility of the Earth. Interestingly, green is similarly connected to death in Greek mythology through the figure of Persephone. Persephone is a daughter of Demeter who represented fertility and growing things, similar to her mother. According to myth, Persephone was abducted by Hades, who took her to the underworld as a captive. While she was there, she was convinced to eat a single pomegranate seed. In eating the fruit of the dead, Persephone became doomed to spend half of the year in the underworld. When Persephone walks the Earth with her mother, green things grow. Yet, when she descends into Hell in the winter, all grows cold and dark. Here again, we have a green growing deity associated with both life and death, a cyclical ritual.

Ingredients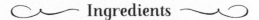

For the Salad

1 cup (200 g) uncooked farro

Salt and pepper, to taste

1 lemon, juiced

1 cucumber, diced

½ cup (75 g) baby tomatoes, halved

½ red onion, diced

1 cup (150 g) roasted red peppers, chopped

1 (14 oz [395 g]) can chickpeas, drained

½ cup (75 g) crumbled feta cheese

For the Vinaigrette

¼ cup (60 ml) extra-virgin olive oil

2 cloves garlic, smashed

2 tbsp (30 ml) lemon juice

1 tsp dried oregano

Salt, to taste

Pepper, to taste

Ancient Farro Salad

Farro has been found in tombs of ancient pharaohs and was said to have fed the Roman legions. It is an ancient grain that originated in the Fertile Crescent, and now grows throughout regions of Italy. Full of nutrients and packed with protein power strong enough to churn civilizations, this is not a grain to be missed.

When you enjoy this salad, you're partaking in a history of food magic that spans the centuries. Combining lots of Greek staples including tomatoes, beans and feta, this salad will transport you back to legends of old. In my imagination, this may be what Calypso served her enchanted guests, as they were lured further and further under her spell.

Serves 2

Prepare the farro based on package directions, until tender. Add salt and pepper to taste. In a large bowl, combine the farro with the juiced lemon, cucumber, baby tomatoes, red onion, roasted red peppers and chickpeas. Top with feta cheese.

To prepare the vinaigrette, combine the olive oil, garlic, lemon juice, oregano and salt in a dressing jar and shake vigorously. For the best flavor, allow this to sit for an hour.

Serve the salad hot or cold, season with pepper and dress with vinaigrette individually, to taste.

Ingredients

2 lbs (907 g) small potatoes

½ cup (120 ml) olive oil

1 tbsp (15 ml) Dijon mustard

1 lemon, juiced

1 tbsp (2 g) fresh thyme leaves

2 tbsp (8 g) fresh parsley, plus more for garnish

2 cloves garlic, minced

¼ tsp pepper

½ tsp salt

Give it Thyme Potato Salad

Across . . . well . . . time, thyme has been associated with bravery. In folk magic, thyme has been used in teas and beverages as a potion to ward against nightmares. It was believed that this courage-inducing herb could seep into a sleeper's mind and fight against the darkness that might lurk there.

In this recipe, thyme is included as a fragrant pairing with parsley and the vibrant zest of lemon. Consider utilizing this hearty salad recipe when you're looking for a little more pluck to prepare for what awaits you. Maybe there's a stressor coming up on the morrow; prepare this recipe for dinner the night before. Remind yourself of the many people before you who have turned to thyme to help them tread boldly forward without fear.

Serves 4

Prepare the potatoes by washing, scrubbing and quartering them. Then, in a large pot, cover the potatoes with water and simmer for 15 minutes, until softened. To prepare the dressing, combine the olive oil, Dijon, lemon juice, thyme, parsley, garlic, pepper and salt, and whisk well.

Cover the cooked potatoes in the dressing and mix well, then serve. This salad may be served hot or cold. Garnish with additional fresh parsley.

Ingredients

5 strips of bacon, cut into small pieces

2 tbsp (30 ml) olive oil

¼ tsp red pepper flakes

1 clove of garlic, diced

3 cups (90 g) fresh spinach

2 cups (40 g) arugula

2 cups (40 g) chard

2 cups (134 g) baby kale

½ cup (80 g) sliced red onion

¼ tsp salt

2 tbsp (30 ml) balsamic vinegar

Wilted Greens Salad

When we look outside in the summer months, we're surrounded by a world growing full of green. There's something magic in this color, so full of life and potential. When I eat greens, I always feel so wholly connected to the earth around me. From my toes to my fingertips, green seems to permeate the very air we breathe.

When creating this salad, I wanted to connect all the potency of greens with the savory comfort of the hearth. Combining heat and greens with some salt and fat, we've concocted a healthful meal packed with all the potencies of Gaia's earthly bounty.

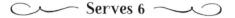 Serves 6

In a pan, cook the bacon until tender. Drain the grease and set the bacon aside. In the same pan, add olive oil, red pepper flakes and garlic. Allow these to cook until fragrant, then add the spinach, arugula, chard and kale. Cook until the greens are just wilted and transfer them to a serving bowl. To the greens, add the cooked bacon (reserving some for garnishing), red onion, salt and balsamic vinegar.

Serve the salad hot, season with salt, and garnish with extra bacon.

CHARCUTERIE CORRESPONDENCES

When I think about a charcuterie board, I imagine friends and family gathered around a table, sharing cocktails and stories together in warm congeniality. There's something so intrinsically bonding about sharing food from the same plate, and charcuterie boards bring out this connection in such a classic and delicious way. When you imagine these same gatherings, who do you see in your mind's eye? A friend, a partner, family?

In this activity, I'll guide you through a simple blessing meant to be shared with the one you love. This blessing can be conducted in privacy, or together with your loved one.

The Ritual: Sending a Blessing

Before you begin this ritual, you'll need to gather two simple items. First, you will need a white candle. White represents purification and cleansing energies, and in magic, white candles can be used to clear away negative energies. Second, you'll need to find a token or object that relates to your loved one. This token object will act as a physical reminder of your loved one, helping you to bring even more powerful energy into the prayer.

To begin the ritual, light the candle and recite the prayer on the following page. Depending on your own beliefs and spirituality, consider directing this prayer to the deity, force or spirit that guides you. If you are agnostic, then proceed with this blessing as a form of meaningful meditation; send all of your love and emotions out into the world for your loved one, and visualize ways that you can actualize this into reality. For all practitioners, it is a wonderful step to move forward from this blessing considering ways in which to extend the blessing through physical acts and services, whether that be a kind phone call or a caring favor.

As you recite the prayer, hold on to your token, and bring it close to your chest. Feel the spirit of your loved one and harness those feelings to form a hug around you. As you close out the prayer, lower the token or object and place it in front of you. Keep the token with you or share it with your loved one, as a gift of appreciation, along with these words:

By the light of the flame that burns before me
I call for a blessing of sacred light
May warmth and happiness rain down upon
[Name]

Let my love extend through the darkness
Like this candle's flame
To reach [Name]
And shower them with comfort

I am blessed to love and be loved by [Name]
May these words echo

To [Name]'s ears and
Bring peace

Ingredients

For the Rosemary-Infused Honey
1 jar of honey

5–6 sprigs of rosemary

For the Baked Brie
1 wheel of brie

2–3 sprigs of rosemary

For the Pansy Syrup
2 cups (400 g) granulated sugar

1 cup (45 g) fresh black or purple pansy flowers

1 cup (240 ml) water

For the Board
1–2 green apples, sliced

1 cup (121 g) dried cranberries

2–3 in (5–8 cm) of Toscana salami, sliced

1 medium slice of Emmental cheese

½ cup (70 g) spicy nut blend

10–15 sesame crackers

5–10 slices of French baguette, lightly toasted

For Garnish
4–5 pansy flowers

2–3 sprigs of rosemary

Convivial Cheese Board

Convivial, as an adjective, refers to a friendly, lively and enjoyable atmosphere or event. I imagine this charcuterie board being served among old friends coming together with laughter and a fast reunion as if time itself has not flown by since the last assembly. In fact, my husband and I are hosting just such a pair of friends as I write this recipe. We're sharing bagels and morning coffee as we discuss the benefits of one cheese over the other for this very board. It's an environment full of its own magic, the magic of connection and harmony amongst people who know you in the best of ways.

The use of rosemary in this board is a special homage to the ideals of friendship and love, with rosemary being a symbol for such. Moreover, rosemary is associated with remembrance. I include this spice in the hopes of crafting a special moment in time that you can capture in your mind to recall when days grow lonely or cold. Not only is this recipe a celebration of the moment, but it is also packed with this sweet-smelling spice to help you recall the moments that you shared over a simple meal of meat, cheese and bread.

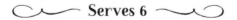 **Serves 6**

For the Rosemary-Infused Honey
Combine the honey and rosemary in a sealable mason jar. Let it sit for up to a week, shaking and tasting periodically throughout. After the preferred flavor is reached, strain out the rosemary and store the honey in the mason jar.

For the Baked Brie
Preheat the oven to 350°F (175°C). Place the brie on a tray and bake for 15 to 20 minutes, or until melted through. Serve with a drizzle of rosemary-infused honey. Top with a decorative sprig of rosemary.

(continued)

For the Green Apples with Pansy Syrup

In a food processor, combine the sugar and pansies (make sure you are using culinary grade flowers). Process the sugar and pansy mixture for about thirty seconds. Then, add the sugar mixture and water to a saucepan. Bring the mixture to a boil, then reduce and simmer it until the liquid becomes syrup (or coats the back of a spoon), about 10 minutes.

Allow the syrup to cool and serve drizzled over apple slices.

For Plating

When preparing a charcuterie board, one of the most important things to keep in mind is color. Be sure to organize the offerings in a way that is visually appealing, whether concentrating color or organizing in a gradual blend of color (a gradient for example). Next, you need to consider the use of texture. Your goal is to invite the eye to move across the board, almost like a painting. Consider the focal points of your board and ensure that these correspond in a natural path for the eye to follow. The beauty of a charcuterie board is first in its appearance and then, its taste.

For this board, the baked brie should be the center of attention. Position the brie in a central place on your board or serving dish, surrounding it with the apple, laying the slices one after the other, slightly overlapping. The pansy syrup should be served in a glass saucer or vial, for pouring. This should also sit next to the apples. I recommend placing the Emmentel cheese and salami on opposite ends of the brie, arranging the other accoutrement around these two focal items. In particular, the cranberries, Toscana salami, spicy nut blend, sesame crackers and French baguette should be arranged in small groupings. If necessary, you can break these up and feature them on multiple locations within the arrangement. For example, you may want to feature the cranberries, in multiple spots for a pop of color. Finally, drizzle the brie with the rosemary-infused honey. Place a few sprigs of rosemary and pansy flowers around the plate, for accessorizing.

A Sumptuous Spread

American writer and poet Dorothy Parker, known for her caustic wit, was once quoted: "Take care of the luxuries, and the necessities will take care of themselves." This recipe is an homage to such sentiments, with loads of deeply rich ingredients and an abundance of decadence. Every piece of this charcuterie board is loaded with flavor, vibrant color and aesthetic value; from the bright red strawberries to creamy mascarpone, this board is a celebration of flavor and beauty.

In some ways, I find charcuterie to be a bit of a spell in and of itself. Reminding me almost of an offering, the appeal of charcuterie is arranging food in a way that appears artisanal and supple. As you prepare this board, consider that it is an offering to yourself from yourself. Enjoy the luxury of such a meal, and in this process, you're simultaneously filling those necessities of hunger and hosting.

Serves 8-10

The same aesthetic instructions apply to this charcuterie board as are listed in the previous recipe. Color is a particular focal point of this spread, especially when it's crafted with lots of varying shades and textures. In addition to the ideals of color and motion, you should also consider an appropriate board for the spread. This recipe features a large variety of ingredients, so it's best to have a large area on which to arrange the charcuterie. In particular, wood or slate would be an appropriate pairing. If utilizing slate, you could consider adding chalk accents to the board upon completion of the arrangement. You could label particular ingredients, or alternatively, add designs such as swirls or arrows.

(continued)

Ingredients

Aged gouda, sliced

Manchego, sliced

4–5 slices prosciutto

10–15 pita crackers

5–10 Croccantini® crackers

5–10 pieces of baguette, toasted

¼ cup (60 ml) blackberry jam

½ cup (116 g) mascarpone cheese, drizzled with honey

¼ cup (60 ml) beer mustard

2–3 pieces dark chocolate

½ cup (83 g) strawberries, sliced

3–4 in (7–10 cm) summer sausage, sliced

5–6 mini dill pickles

1 cup (151 g) purple grapes

¼ cup (45 g) green olives stuffed with feta

½ cup (72 g) Marcona almonds

¼ cup (31 g) pistachios

Evening

To begin arranging this piece, I recommend placing the cheeses and meats at equal intervals, alternating between meat and cheese. For example, placing the gouda cheese near the end of the tray, then 2 inches (5 cm) away, placing the prosciutto. Around the cheeses, place some cracker and baguette options, keeping the arrangement elegant. As you place the crackers, layer them so that one sits slightly over the next, in a fan-like arrangement.

Next, place the dressings and toppings onto the platter, in appropriate serving dishes. For example, the blackberry jam could be placed in a small glass jar, with a small teaspoon for serving.

Once the cheeses, crackers and toppings are arranged on the plate, place the remaining ingredients, grouping like with like. I would recommend keeping similar or complementary flavors together. For example, place the chocolate pieces near the strawberries.

Finally, consider the final board and ensure that every ingredient is laid out in an aesthetically pleasing and organized manner. The goal is for this board to look like a sprawling and wild spread, but with synchronicity and vision.

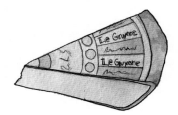

Ingredients

For the
Yogurt Fruit Dip

1 cup (240 ml) plain vanilla
yogurt

2 tbsp (30 ml) honey

½ tsp vanilla extract

¼ cup (35 g) pomegranate
seeds

For the Board

¼ cup (70 g) chocolate
hazelnut spread

20–30 pretzel sticks

1 apple, sliced

5–10 strawberries, stems
removed

½ cup (77 g) black cherries,
pitted

5–10 vanilla wafer cookies

Comfort & Care Carousel

They say a spoonful of sugar helps the medicine go down, but in this recipe the medicine itself is sugary sweet to begin with. Featuring a bounty of fresh fruit, and paired with decadent hazelnut spread and a light yogurt dip, this charcuterie board is perfect for when you're needing a natural pick-me-up.

Nature's own confectionary, cherry features prominently on this board. In Chinese folklore, it was believed that the phoenix slept on a bed of cherry blossoms. This blushing bower is what was purported to gift the phoenix with its ever lasting cycle of life and regeneration. Envision this recipe as the bower on which you too, can rest your head to replenish vitality in your everyday life.

Serves 4

For the yogurt fruit dip, combine yogurt, honey and vanilla extract in a bowl. Mix well. Top the yogurt mixture with pomegranate seeds.

To prepare the charcuterie, place the chocolate hazelnut spread and yogurt dip on opposite ends of the platter. Arrange the remainder of the ingredients around these dishes in a pleasant and aesthetically engaging manner.

HOSTING A SLEEPY HOLLOW SOIRÉE

When I envision Sleepy Hollow, images of headless horsemen and roaming ghouls fill my mind's eye. I'm lost, awash in the words of famous author and folklorist Washington Irving: "There is nothing like the silence and loneliness of night to bring dark shadows over the brightest mind." Just as shadows fill the mind with reveries of hauntings, so too will this soirée fill the minds of guests with their favorite spooky story.

The Ritual: Sharing Frights

In this ritual, I recommend hosting an extension of the folk practice of scary story sharing. All that I am suggesting, simply put, is to set aside time during this organized soirée for guests to tell their best scary story, fact or fiction.

Now, you might think, "This isn't a ritual at all!" Well, I would argue that this is one of the oldest rituals in which you can partake when sharing time together. Just imagine cavemen in their dens, painting stories of the hunt on their cave walls and reminiscing about all the close calls they encountered with some saber-toothed tiger. This is what it means to be human! Sharing connection through our fears is a universal and well-practiced ritual that has given rise to some of the most famous horror stories to date.

Evening

Famously, the lauded novel of *Frankenstein* was written by Mary Shelley as part of a competition between herself, Percy Shelley, John William Polidori and Lord Byron to see who could write the best horror story. From that simple contest, came both the final novels of *Frankenstein* and Polidori's *The Vampyre*, an originating vampire myth. These classics of horror came about because a group of people were lounging around together in Switzerland, entertaining themselves in this ancient ritual of sharing what frightens us!

As you prepare this feast and await your guests, I urge you to reach into those cobwebbed corners of your mind where fear resides. What story might you share when all eyes turn to you?

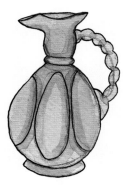

Ingredients

1 gallon (3.8 L) of beer

8 cups (2 quarts) orange juice

Small Beer

In the archaic definition of the word, small beer refers to a weak or light beer. In colonial America, the term small beer was generally used to refer to home brews, which were lower in alcohol content. These weaker beers were socially popular because a person could drink a few glasses subsequently without suffering the effects of an overindulgence of alcohol.

For this Sleepy Hollow Soirée, this small beer cocktail will be a perfect pairing for Katrina's Candied Citrus (page 117) and other such dishes. Moreover, the addition of orange adds a symbolic encouragement to engage in lively conversation and socialization. I imagine that even the stuttering Ichabod Crane would open up over a nice cup of this delightful, yet delicate, elixir.

 Serves 8

Pour the beer into a frosted stein and then add the orange juice. Mix lightly and enjoy the cold refreshment.

Note: This is a delightfully easy recipe, with an extensive batch of variations and potential adjustments, for any flavor palette. Starting out, I'd recommend a light beer for this recipe. Some brands in particular that come to mind are Oberon® and Blue Moon®. However, feel free to be creative with your beer selection and go with what tastes best to you. Keep in mind that the main flavor profile will be featuring a heavy citrus, so beers like sours, lagers, and IPAs will act as more natural companions than say, a stout. Lastly, feel free to experiment with the ratio of juice to beer. In this recipe, I recommend 1/3 juice to 2/3 beer. However, some may find that they prefer a varied ratio one way or another.

Ingredients

1 package (7 g) fresh yeast

1⅓ cup (320 ml) warm water

⅓ cup (66 g) sugar

⅓ cup (75 g) lard

1 tsp salt

4 cups (500 g) flour, divided

½ cup (114 g) butter, for topping

Old-Fashioned Yeast Rolls

The magic of bread is the magic of smell, nostalgia and home. For these rolls, I'm pulling from my own family traditions featuring a recipe handed down from my great-aunt to my mother, to me (as inherited recipes are wont to travel). Primarily staples of our Thanksgiving table, these rolls were greedily hoarded by my childhood self and my red-cheeked cousins as we ran from the kitchen to the patio, where we sat on miniature wicker chairs, chewing merrily the favorite food of that feast day.

Traditionally baked on the very stones of a hearth, bread in the colonial era was a staple of diets for peasant folk. In Sleepy Hollow, I imagine that no feast would be complete without some hearty traditional yeast rolls. Smelling of tangy fresh yeast and topped with rich butter, this bread is loaded with the tastes of yesteryear.

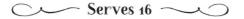 Serves 16

Dissolve the yeast in the warm water and let sit it for about 10 minutes. Then, add in the sugar, lard and salt. Next, add 2 cups (250 g) of the flour and stir well. Add 2 more cups (250 g) of the flour gradually (adding in an additional ½ cup [63 g] if the dough is too sticky). Leave the dough mixture in its bowl on a counter, covered with a dish towel, and allow it to rise for 1 hour.

Punch down the dough, cover and place it in the refrigerator to rise for at least 1 more hour. Remove the dough from the refrigerator about 3 hours before you're ready to serve the rolls. Often, I prepare this dough a day before I need the rolls, so the dough can rise overnight in the fridge as necessary.

Shape the dough into rolls and let them rise on a counter, covered, for about 3 hours, or until doubled in size. Bake at 400°F (200 °C) for about 10 minutes, or until browned. After the rolls have baked, top them with a light layer of butter while warm, then let cool (or, carefully, indulge in one fresh from the oven!).

Ingredients

2–3 tbsp (30–45 ml) olive oil

3–5-lb (1½–2¼-kg) chuck roast

1 onion, peeled and halved

5–6 carrots, sliced

2 stalks celery

1 cup (240 ml) red wine

1 lb (454 g) baby potatoes

3 cups (720 ml) beef broth

½ tsp dried rosemary

½ tsp thyme

1 bay leaf

Salt and pepper, to taste

Fresh rosemary, for garnish

Drunken Pot Roast

Washington Irving writes, at the conclusion of his fabled tale "The Legend of Sleepy Hollow": "The storyteller, who was just putting a glass of wine to his lips, as a refreshment after his toils, pauses . . ." Thus, signifying that just as the story was written out to us, he heard from the lips of a wine-drinking "storyteller." As you see, wine is deeply intertwined within this tale of haunts and goblins.

Appropriately, rich red wine flavors this decadent and hearty pot roast, the centerpiece for a celebration full of spooky solemnity. My general recommendation for a wine to use in this dish is one that is deep and full-bodied, such as a Cabernet Franc or rich merlot.

Serves 8

Preheat the oven to 275°F (135°C).

Add the olive oil into a Dutch oven and allow it to heat. Once the pot is hot, add the chuck roast and brown on both sides. Transfer the roast to a plate. Similarly, sear the onion and transfer it to a separate plate. Add more oil if necessary, and then place the carrots and celery in the Dutch oven and mix them around until lightly browned. Remove them and set aside with the onion.

Lower the heat and add the red wine to the Dutch oven, whisking to deglaze. Then, add back the browned chuck roast, onion, carrots and celery and add the baby potatoes. Pour the beef broth over the chuck roast until it is partially submerged. Then, add the rosemary, thyme, bay leaf and salt and pepper to taste.

Put the lid on the Dutch oven and allow it to roast for an hour per pound (about 2 hours per kg) of roast.

Once the meat has roasted and become tender, pull it apart and serve with the onion, carrots, celery and potatoes. Garnish with fresh rosemary.

Ingredients

½ cup (120 ml) sour cream

½ tbsp (7 ml) Dijon mustard

3 tbsp (35 g) prepared horseradish

3–4 sprigs of chive, finely chopped

Salt and pepper, to taste

Headless Horseradish Sauce

Horseradish is a tough and durable plant that will grow bright green shoots above ground. Below the surface of the Earth, this vegetable burrows deeply with trails of horizontal tubers growing wide and strong. The flavor of these roots is rich and exceedingly spicy, despite the plant's simple appearance in the sunlit garden.

I imagine horseradish would be a flavor that might put off the delicate sensibilities of Ichabod Crane. However, the spice and fire of this sauce reminds me perfectly of the firing pumpkins hurled onward by a wild and craven Headless Horseman.

Serves 8

Combine the sour cream, Dijon, horseradish, chive, salt and pepper to a bowl. Mix well and store in the refrigerator for up to 2 hours. Before serving, garnish with additional chive. This sauce would go well with any pork or beef, and is exceptional when paired with the Drunken Pot Roast (page 113).

Ingredients

1 orange, for zesting

⅓ cup (66 g) sugar

¼ cup (60 ml) orange juice

¼ cup (60 ml) blood orange juice

1 cinnamon stick

3 blood oranges, cut in horizontal slices

5 oranges, cut in horizontal slices

Pomegranate seeds, for garnish

Katrina's Candied Citrus

The orange represents generosity and love in much folklore. During the time of Sleepy Hollow's tale, oranges wouldn't have been common in the colonies. However, I imagine that the magical heroine Katrina Van Tassel would have been a lover of their vibrant colors and citrusy sweet flavors.

In this recipe, we combine the lightly rich flavors of caramel with the deep red berry flavor of blood orange and pomegranate. A celebration of color, this dish represents a gift to those who will indulge in its decadence.

Serves 8

Peel a strip of zest from one orange and add this to a pot of boiling water for about 1 minute. Drain and set the strip of zest aside.

In a saucepan, melt the sugar over medium heat until it has taken on a light brown color. Then, slowly add in the orange juices. The mixture will bubble and condense quickly, but let it simmer and the blend will settle. Add the reserved orange zest and cinnamon stick, then allow everything to simmer for 5 minutes or until the sugar has dissolved.

Lastly, add in the sliced oranges and mix gently. Then, pour the sugar and citrus mixture onto a plate and let it cool in the fridge. Serve garnished with pomegranate seeds.

Night

"Those who dream by day are cognizant of many things which escape those who dream only by night."

–Edgar Allan Poe, "Eleonora"

All the Earth is nestled down within its bedding, waiting for the stars to dance above, swooning lullabies echo across time. At night, we find ourselves searching the shadows of our mind, sometimes lazily and other times anxiously, with the hope we see something more through a lens of darkened meditation. Night might be when we leap through the flames and dance in the grove. Night might be when we hold our lovers close. Night holds the potential for all these vignettes of the human experience, and it is infused with the deepest violet magic.

As I settle into the lull where evening turns to something darker, I might pour myself a nightcap to go along with some light reading. After a while, with heavy eyes, I turn toward bed, maybe lighting a candle to set a serene mood within my room. As scents of lavender, or maybe mint, waft delicately across my pillow, I finally succumb to the siren call of sleep. Snuffing out the candle, dreams overtake me with gentle arms guiding toward fairyland. This evening I've painted is certainly idealized, yet also so simple in its composition.

Night

I believe night is one of those rare moments when we have a certain level of independence. While partners or family may linger close by, there's a welcome isolation to the end of day where you're left alone with your thoughts, desires and emotions.

Every night provides a unique opportunity to reconnect with yourself on a sincere level. Whether you spend the entire evening alone or find silence only in the few minutes before sleeping, there's an opportunity for poignant self-care and meditative magic. In this section, I provide recipes that can aid in the pursuit of individual pleasure and independent craft. Serve yourself a piece of cake, and revel in the luxury of this simple act of personal devotion. Craft an absinthe cocktail to sip and enjoy as you daydream about the green fairy of legend. Anoint a candle and practice candle magic, searching through your intention to increase love, luck or wealth. All of these whimsical practices will pair perfectly with nighttime silence and magic, transporting you into a deeper connection with the darkest turn of the day.

Night Meditation

Here I am in this moment
Surrounded by silence
And glistening starlight
May it fill me with serenity

As the moon blooms above
So too let my mind blossom
As the moon flower
To wonder and dream

May the night pass in peace
And may my sleep be calm
As waves against the shore
May my mind be lulled to rest

COCKTAIL ELIXIRS FOR
POTENT POTION MAKING

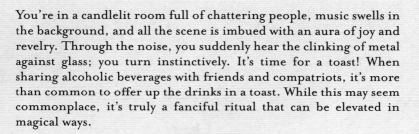

You're in a candlelit room full of chattering people, music swells in the background, and all the scene is imbued with an aura of joy and revelry. Through the noise, you suddenly hear the clinking of metal against glass; you turn instinctively. It's time for a toast! When sharing alcoholic beverages with friends and compatriots, it's more than common to offer up the drinks in a toast. While this may seem commonplace, it's truly a fanciful ritual that can be elevated in magical ways.

According to some questionable stories (the best are often only half true), toasting became a custom to test for poisoned beverages. It was said that by clinking glasses together, some liquid from both would spill into the other, thus proving your drinking partner meant you no ill intent. Based on other sources, the story goes that toasting is a remaining vestige from the days of ancient sacrificial libations. Blood or wine was placed in a ceremonial cup for some deity, and a prayer was sent up, asking for the granting of long life or health.

Whatever the origin of this custom may be, it is now thoroughly enshrined in our culture as a just and right way to share goodwill among companions. In this activity, I will share a few tried and true toasts for you to enjoy with friends and family. These toasts are perfect to pair with the following recipes—may you never drink alone!

Night

The Ritual: Toasting Traditions

For this ritual, all you need to gather are some friends and delicious beverages. As is the toasting tradition, one person will call for a toast either by clinking their glass with the dull end of a knife, or simply stating they "call for a toast." Raise your glass as you recite the preferred toast, and then be sure to take a drink after clinking glasses with all in attendance. Don't forget, it's bad luck if you forget to drink after a toast!

This first toast features the common Irish blessing, which emphasizes goodwill toward a person who may be taking a journey or making a life change. I recommended this toast for when a friend may be going on a trip, starting a new venture or moving.

May the road rise to meet you.
May the wind be always at your back.
May the sun shine warm upon your face.
And rains fall soft upon your fields.
And until we meet again,
May God hold you in the hollow of His hand.

For a less serious toast, consider the words of F. Scott Fitzgerald, "Here's to alcohol, the rose-colored glasses of life." While there are toasts for any occasion, there are also many toasts to celebrate the act of imbibing itself. Some of the best toasts, in my opinion, are a little bit tongue in cheek and feature some whimsical free verse poetry. For example, consider this toast to friendship and debauchery: "One bottle for the four of us, thank God there are no more of us!"

Finally, I have to share a hobbit-inspired toast, written by J.R.R. Tolkien, which is perfect for a raucous gathering, especially for a rip-roaring "eleventy-first" birthday party:

"Ho, ho, ho! To the bottle I go
To heal my heart and drown my woe
Rain may fall, and wind may blow
And many miles be still to go
But under a tall tree will I lie
And let the clouds go sailing by."

Ingredients

8 cups (2 L) apple cider

2 cups (480 ml) orange juice

1 cup (240 ml) pineapple juice

4 cinnamon sticks

12 whole cloves

¼ tsp ground ginger

¼ tsp nutmeg

1 cup (240 ml) rum

Wassail

The verb wassailing is an archaic term referring to the indulgence of alcohol and merry making among friends, while traveling door to door singing and reveling in exchange for gifts of money and baked goods. Often, groups would go "wassailing" around Twelfth Night in the wintertime as part of ritual celebrations for the season. Today, we know caroling as the evolution of this more ancient tradition. In the hand of every wassailer would be a warming glass of potent and flavorful wassail.

This beverage features the Yuletide flavors of cinnamon, clove and orange, embodying the very generosity within gifts of orange balms and spices. While indulging in this wassail, consider the way in which this elixir represents friendship and common kindness.

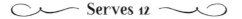 Serves 12

Combine the apple cider, orange juice, pineapple juice, cinnamon sticks, cloves, ginger, nutmeg and rum in a large pot and bring to a boil. Allow the mixture to simmer for 45 minutes, or until the flavors are well combined. Stir frequently and serve warm.

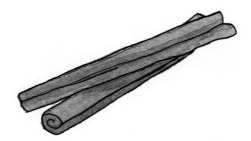

Ingredients

For the Lavender Simple Syrup

½ cup (100 g) sugar

½ cup (120 ml) water

1 tbsp (6 g) fresh lavender flowers

For the Garden Gimlet

2½ oz (73 ml) gin

½ oz (15 ml) freshly squeezed lime juice

½ oz (15 ml) lavender simple syrup

Lime wheel, for garnish

Garden Gimlet

Gin is a beautiful spirit, full of botanical notes and resonances from the herb garden. This gimlet accentuates the flavor of lavender with the inclusion of a simple lavender syrup brewed with fresh lavender flowers. Symbolically, lavender represents purity, silence, devotion, serenity, grace and calmness.

As you indulge in this beverage, consider closing your eyes and relaxing into a meditative state for a moment. Allow the delicate alcohol to transport your mind and palate to a twilight garden, where all is calm and cloaked in purple shadows.

When sourcing your lavender for this recipe, be certain to select a culinary grade lavender flower.

Serves 1
with extra lavender simple syrup

First prepare the lavender simple syrup. Combine the sugar, water and lavender flowers in a saucepan and bring to a simmer. Once the sugar has dissolved and the mixture has thickened, remove the syrup from the heat. Allow it to sit for 30 minutes while the flavors settle. Then, strain and pour the syrup into an airtight container. Store it in the fridge for later use.

To make the Garden Gimlet, combine the gin, lime juice and simple syrup in a shaker with ice. Shake well and strain the gimlet into a chilled cocktail glass. Garnish with a lime wheel.

Ingredients

For the Elderflower Syrup

½ cup (120 ml) water

½ cup (100 g) sugar

1 tbsp (6 g) fresh elderflowers

For the Mystical Mule

1½ oz (44 ml) vodka

½ oz (15 ml) lime juice

Ice cubes

½ cup (120 ml) ginger beer

1 tsp elderflower syrup

Elderberries, for garnish

Mystical Mule

The elder tree is full of magic and folkloric connections. Varying myths around Europe and Scandinavia involve the use of elder branches, flowers and berries to connect with fae, protect from evil and even cure toothaches. My personal favorite elder tale goes like this: If you stand beneath the boughs of an elder tree on Midsummer's Eve, then you might be granted sight through the veil, and you'll witness the Elf King and his host of fairies, goblins and sprites.

In this mystical mule, vodka combines with sweet elderflower syrup and tangy ginger beer to create a frothing beverage perfect for Midsummer's Eve or any special occasion. Consider leaving a small tipple behind in a thimble for the fairies to bless your home and garden.

When selecting your elderflowers for this recipe, ensure that you're choosing a flower of culinary grade.

Serves 2
with extra elderflower syrup

First prepare the elderflower simple syrup. Combine the sugar, water and elderflowers in a saucepan and bring to a simmer. Once the sugar has dissolved and the mixture has thickened, remove the syrup from the heat. Allow it to sit for 30 minutes while the flavors settle. Then, strain and pour it into an airtight container. Store the syrup in the fridge for later use.

To prepare the Mystical Mule, combine all the ingredients in a pitcher and mix. Pour the mules into two copper mugs and enjoy cold, garnished with elderberries.

1 oz (30 ml) absinthe

1 oz (30 ml) lemon juice

¾ oz (22 ml) rose water

¾ oz (22 ml) pineapple juice

Absinthe Cocktail

Referred to in historical literature as "la fée verte," or "The Green Fairy," absinthe is a spirit derived from several medicinal plants including grand wormwood, anise and sweet fennel. According to some common myth (though not substantiated by the weighty burden of truth), absinthe could cause a drinker to fall into bouts of hallucinogenic madness, witnessing the green fairy and falling prey to artistic ennui.

In reality, absinthe is simply a beverage with high alcohol content. When drunk in moderation, the imbiber is more than safe from fairy sightings. This cocktail combines the whimsical flavors of absinthe with garden-paired rose water, and a bite of citrus from lemon and pineapple. As you enjoy this beverage, take note of its opalescent color, and indulge in its decadence. Know you're drinking in good company, as this is a delicacy once prized by artists Ernest Hemingway, Lewis Carroll, Oscar Wilde and French composer Erik Satie.

⌒⌒ Serves 1 ⌒⌒

Add the absinthe, lemon juice, rose water and pineapple juice to a shaker with ice and shake until cold. Pour the cocktail into a coupe glass prepared with one large stone of ice.

DECADENT DESSERTS FOR RITUAL ROMANCE & SELF-LOVE

Just before writing this, I ate cake for breakfast, and it was a delicious way to start the day. There's something so decadent about serving yourself a piece of cake, and it's especially true when you forgo common cultural customs such as "breakfast-appropriate" foods. In this section, I share three delightful dessert recipes that are meant to feel like an indulgence.

When thinking about a ritual to pair with these recipes, I kept coming back to the idea of spoiling yourself through acts of radical self-love. Finally, what came to mind when considering these ideals was the ritual of a magical bath. Magical baths can follow one of two paths: You can create a bath with the intention of absorbing energy or of cleansing energy. When I say energies, I am talking about emotions, thoughts and symbolically significant experiences. Through meditation, magical elements and simple water, you're conducting your own personal ritual of renewal and self-care.

The Ritual: Soaking in Sweetness

To prepare this bath, you'll need to gather some oils, herbs and stones that resonate with you and your own preferences. Consider elements from the list on the next page and note each item's correspondences. Feel free to play around with the symbolism of this bath, catering it toward what you feel you need to soak in at this moment in time.

Night

Essential Oils:

Chamomile - happiness, tranquility, purification
Lavender - calm, serenity, devotion, grace
Rose - romance, love, beauty, courage

Herbs:

Peppermint - virtue, hospitality
Ginger - strength, warmth, vitality

Crystals:

Clear Quartz - mental clarity
Green Aventurine - inner peace, promoting spiritual growth
Black Onyx - grounding, protection, self-control

When preparing the materials for your bath, consider health and safety first. Before using a new material in your bath time ritual, spot test them on your skin and wait 24 hours to ensure you're not sensitive to an ingredient.

After you've gathered the supplies for your bath, run the water to a preferred temperature. When the tub has filled, combine a few drops of your essential oil with a small amount of a carrier oil like coconut or jojoba oil and add them to the bath—a little goes a long way. Next, place your herbs and crystals into a cloth sachet and add the sachet to the tub as well. If you're uncertain whether a particular crystal is water safe, then air on the side of caution and simply place it near the tub in a meaningful way.

Now it's time to step in and soak up all the delightful scents and energies you've combined for yourself. While bathing, close your eyes and practice some light meditation. Focus on the aroma in the air and the buoyancy of your body. Consider reciting a self-love mantra: "I am worthy" or "I love myself." As the water cools, allow yourself to arise from meditation and luxuriate in the bath until you're ready to close the ritual.

As you leave the tub, dry off gently and rub any remaining oils into your skin. Allow the scent to remind you of all the warmth and positive energies that you've soaked up throughout the ritual.

Ingredients

1 cup (125 g) flour

¼ tsp salt

2 tsp (9 g) baking powder

1 tbsp (14 g) butter

⅓ cup (80 ml) milk

1 egg, well-beaten

1 apple

2 tbsp (16 g) granulated sugar

½ tsp cinnamon

Cinnamon Cake for the Working Witch

I've pulled this particular recipe from a cookbook written in 1917 by Louise Bennett Weaver and Helen Cowles LeCron. It's an old recipe, tried and true, for people who are busy with lots of life to live. As they advertise in the book, it's simple and sweet—perfect, I think, for a working Witch!

One of my favorite things about this recipe is its inclusion of apples and sugar as a topping. Caramelized in the oven, these ingredients turn in to the perfect crust. Enjoy this with a side of whipped cream or ice cream. I recommend this recipe for those days when you may be expecting a somewhat surprise guest. Simple to make and perfectly hospitable, cinnamon creates an aura of welcome that surely will not go unnoticed.

Serves 12

Preheat the oven to 350°F (175°C). In a bowl, mix the flour, salt and baking powder, then cut in the butter. In a separate bowl, combine the milk and egg. Then, pour the wet mixture into the dry mixture and blend until smooth. Pour the mix into an 8-inch [20-cm] circular cake tin.

Then, pare the apple and cut it into thin lengthwise slices. Arrange these slices on top of your batter in an aesthetically pleasing manner. Mix the sugar and cinnamon together, then sprinkle the mix on top of the cake batter and apples.

Bake for 30 minutes or until a toothpick comes out clean.

Ingredients

⅓ lb (150 g) walnuts

¼ lb (114 g) almonds

¼ lb (114 g) peanuts

⅛ lb (55 g) pistachios

1 tsp ground cinnamon

16 oz (454 g) phyllo dough

1 cup (227 g) butter

1 cup (200 g) granulated sugar

1 cup (240 ml) water

½ cup (120 ml) honey

1 tsp vanilla extract

Honeybee Baklava

Honeybees carry so much symbolism—with tiny wings they flit from flower to flower, beautiful yet carrying the threat of a sting if mistreated. Honeybees are a collective, working together for the greater good. In some instances, they may symbolize abundance, cohesion and fortitude; in others, they may signify hidden power or disguised danger.

In this recipe, we utilize sweet honey to flavor a deeply rich baklava. Full of nutty fat and rich butter, this dessert is powerfully potent and should be served sparingly. A little goes a long way.

Serves 16

Preheat the oven to 350°F (175°C). Chop the nuts in a food processor until well broken up and add in the cinnamon, mixing well. Then, unroll your phyllo dough and cover it with a damp towel to keep it moist.

Grease a 9 x 13-inch pan (23 x 33-cm) well with butter and begin to layer your baklava, starting with the phyllo dough. Place two sheets of phyllo dough in the pan and cover with butter, then top with the nut and cinnamon mixture. Repeat this step until you've created 6 to 8 layers. For the top layer, add two more sheets of phyllo dough and cover with butter.

Cut the baklava into diamonds by slicing diagonals across and through the pan. Be sure to cut to the very bottom of the pan as you go. Then, bake the baklava for about 50 minutes, until golden and crisp.

While the baklava bakes, prepare your syrup topping. In a saucepan, combine the sugar and water and bring to a boil. Allow to simmer for 5 to 10 minutes until slightly thickened. Add honey and vanilla, then set aside.

Remove the baklava from the oven and pour the syrup over it immediately. Allow to cool before serving.

Ingredients

¾ cup (168 g) unsalted butter,
plus more for greasing pan

12 oz (340 g) bittersweet chocolate, chopped

6 large eggs

½ cup (100 g) granulated sugar

1 tsp vanilla extract

1 tsp salt

Powdered sugar, for garnish

Raspberries, for garnish

Dark Chocolate Torte

In magic, chocolate is a binding ingredient full of passionate and loving energies. Just as chocolate is an aphrodisiac in the culinary world, so too is it associated with romance in folk magic. As you create this cake, especially while melting down the chocolate, consider reciting some loving statements to yourself, as a ritual of self-care and compassion. You know best what you need to hear, so follow your intuition when crafting these simple statements.

As an ultimate act of self-love and prioritizing personal reverence, consider serving yourself the first piece of this torte. Traditionally, we honor someone by giving them the first slice of a celebratory cake. In this reversal, you're baking and serving yourself as a sign that you honor yourself in an intimate way.

Serves 12

Preheat the oven to 350°F (175°C). Combine the butter and chocolate in a heat-proof bowl, and place the bowl over a saucepan with simmering water. Allow the butter and chocolate to melt and combine, mixing occasionally. Once blended, remove from the heat.

In another bowl, combine the eggs, sugar, vanilla and salt. Beat well for 5 to 10 minutes until pale and thick. Gently fold the chocolate mixture into the egg mixture until combined.

Prepare a 9-inch (23-cm) springform pan with butter, then pour the torte mixture into the pan. Bake for 45 to 50 minutes, or until a toothpick inserted into the center comes out mostly clean. Remove the ring from the springform pan and allow the torte to cool. Once cooled, top with powdered sugar and serve with raspberries for garnish.

OIL INFUSIONS FOR VARIETAL MAGIC

Oil is a powerful conduit, utilized throughout various spiritual practices for purposes from cooking to anointing. In this section, we're developing infused oils that will add flavor and intention to a variety of dishes with their hearty herbal notes and flavors. Not only will these oils provide magic in the kitchen, but they can be transferred into other rituals as well. In particular, these oils are perfectly prepared for inclusion in candle magic.

"Candle magic" is the practice of utilizing a candle within spell making and ritual. The candle acts as a poignant conduit, symbolizing all four elements with its burning. The flame represents fire, air feeds the flame, hot wax symbolizes the water element, and dry wax represents earth. Candle magic can be adjusted and maneuvered to fit a variety of intentions, with techniques such as selecting a particular colored candle; carving sigils into the candle; and anointing the candle with special oils. In this section, I will recommend candle pairings for practice with the three oil infusions. Utilizing these oils within candle magic is another way of setting clear intentions and moving them forward into reality with the help of a visual signifier of your desires.

The Ritual: Anointing Candle Magic

Each of the three oils that we create in this section have their own symbolic focus. One is for wish fulfillment, another is for abundance or money magic, and the last is for romance. To work with each of these using candle magic, I would recommend a similar ritual with a few varying pieces and mantras. However, the general format for the ritual will remain the same.

For a wish fulfillment ritual, I would recommend anointing an orange candle with the oil infusion for wishes (page 141). Orange represents ambition and helps to guide your energies towards fulfillment of a goal or idea. In this way, you're combining the idea of your wish with practical feet-on-the-ground momentum. As you light the candle, focus on the flame, and consider your wish in your mind. Begin to imagine the steps forward that will help to bring your wish into reality. Practice steady breathing with the mantra "I can achieve this wish, it is only a matter of time."

For a money magic ritual, I would recommend anointing a green candle with the oil infusion for money magic (page 143). The green candle helps to bring ideas to life, and aids in prosperity. Green is also commonly associated with currency, so this amplifies the ideals of bringing more money into your life. While the candle burns, envision yourself surrounded by abundance and full of gratitude. Depending on your current situation, consider the following mantras: "I deserve abundance of all kinds," or "My financial fate is not set in stone."

Finally, for a romance magic ritual, I would recommend anointing a red candle with the oil infusion for romance (page 145). A red candle represents love, passion and erotic energy. When lighting a red candle, consider the relationship in your life that is at the center of your intention. While the candle burns, consider the ways in which you might nurture this relationship. Consider the warmth that you yourself feel within the context of you and your romantic attachment. If you're struggling to find love or you're searching for love, then consider ways to celebrate yourself. Think of the relationship you hope to have and consider how you're preparing yourself for that future. For this ritual, some mantras that may serve are as follows: "I am deserving of love," "I celebrate the love in my life," and "May love fill my hours."

Finally, at the conclusion of your candle ritual, remember one important magical rule. Do not blow out the candle with your own breath, as this symbolizes pushing away the intentions that you've been meditating on. Instead, allow the candle to burn out on its own, or snuff it out with a tool.

Ingredients

½ cup (40 g) fresh sage leaves

2 cups (475 ml) extra-virgin olive oil

Oil Infusion for Wishes

To bring a wish to fruition, it is said that you should write your wish on a sage leaf and sleep with it under your pillow for three days. Not only will your wish be granted, but your dreams will be blessed with visions of your wish in its fulfillment. In this oil, we combine the whimsical, wish-granting sage and rich olive oil to create a potent infusion for boosting wish-making magic.

Consider using this oil with your cooked spells or rituals involving the ideals of goals, hopes and intentions. As you pour in the oil, consider your wish, and begin to identify the way in which this wish may become reality. Utilize sage's boosting energies to create goals and focus on the path towards that which you seek.

Yields 16 oz (475 ml)

Cut the sage leaves and combine them with the olive oil in a clean airtight container. Allow the mixture to sit for 2 to 3 weeks and then taste for flavor. When the infusion is to your liking, strain the sage leaves and store the remaining oil in a fresh clean jar.

Ingredients

2 cups (475 ml) extra-virgin olive oil

½ cup (40 g) basil leaves, stems removed

1 clove of garlic

Oil Infusion for Money Magic

Carrying basil in your pocket is said to attract wealth, but in this recipe, we're carrying the basil in our oil with the same intention. Basil is associated with prosperity and abundance, so it makes the perfect ingredient for this money magic infusion.

When you utilize this oil, consider both the abundance you're yearning for and the prosperity you already have. Take a moment to say thanks in gratitude before envisioning the blessings you hope will become endowed upon you. For extra flair, consider adorning the container with lucky pennies as decoration.

Yields 16 oz (475 ml)

Add the olive oil, basil and garlic to a food processor and blend until combined. Then, add the mixture to a saucepan and bring it to a boil, simmering for about a minute.

Remove the oil from the heat and strain it through a fine-mesh strainer or chinois. Strain one last time through a paper coffee filter into a medium-sized bowl. Allow the mixture to sit for 2 hours, then pour into an airtight container for storage.

Ingredients

2 cups (475 ml) extra-virgin olive oil,
or melted coconut oil

3 oz (85 g) fresh turmeric, grated

3 oz (85 g) fresh ginger, grated

Oil Infusion for Romance

Ginger is an ingredient that adds heat and spice to any recipe, warming the body and bringing a flush to the cheeks. In a love potion, ginger adds passion and zest. Combining ginger with the flavorful spice of turmeric, this infusion is ready for any date night meal, emphasizing romantic love and cozy emotions.

Ginger is also associated symbolically with healing, so this oil could be utilized as a kind of healing spell for the broken-hearted. If you're utilizing the oil in this way, consider the alteration of this love potion into a self-love potion. Allow the warmth to fill your chest and heart, like a hug from within.

Yields 16 oz (475 ml)

Place the olive oil, turmeric and ginger into a saucepan and bring it to a boil, then simmer for 5 minutes. Remove the oil from the heat and allow it to cool slightly, then strain through a fine-mesh strainer into an airtight container.

CLEANSING YOUR KITCHEN
WITH BELL MAGIC

You've just finished a delicious meal with family and friends, and enjoyed hours of laughter and candlelight with a perfectly paired menu. Now, empty glasses are polished and put away, the final guest has made their leave, and you're drying your hands on a soft dish towel. This space has served a magnificent and divine purpose, feeding and housing you and your loved ones. You don't want that feeling to leave, but it's time to close up shop for the night. This is the perfect moment to practice a cleansing ritual, as a way of saying "thank you" to the rooms that hold such sacred meaning in your day-to-day life. In this ritual, we'll explore the practice of sound cleansing, using simple tools that you can integrate into your kitchen and dining space naturally and beautifully.

The Ritual: Ringing Out the Night

The practice of using sound for cleansing and meditative purposes is primordial and can be traced back thousands of years to the use of singing bowls, which have been found across ancient Mesopotamia. These instruments of meditation made their way to regions of Tibet, Nepal and India where they became popularized for introspection and healing. Contemporarily, practices such as sound bathing are re-emerging. They utilize singing bowls and the philosophies behind sound cleansing. While many of these rituals invoke ideologies adopted from the originating regions of these sound practices, there is a universalism about the connection between music and spirituality. Sound has a way of elevating experiences to a new level, where we're able to connect synapses in our mind that otherwise would go separate and stagnant. With the magic of sound, we can move beyond the mundane and into the divine. Working with sound, you can enhance your own desires and intentions to create an environment for your higher needs.

For this ritual, it is best to select an instrument that fits within the theme and aesthetic of your current cooking and dining space. One option, which possesses many positive correspondences and bountiful properties, is the simple brass bell. Brass is a metal that has long symbolized abundance and wealth, being valued in antiquity for currency and jewels. In music, brass is a premium metal for instrument making, valued for its clean tonal properties. However, you should select whatever works the best for you; an instrument can be as simple as a glass that rings when you delicately tap it.

ACKNOWLEDGMENTS

I would like to thank Page Street Publishing for their initiative, guidance and support throughout the creation of this book. I want to send an exceptional thank you to my editor, Madeline Greenhalgh, for her vision and creativity in the development of this work.

I must send a heartfelt thanks to Meg Baskis, Rosie Stewart and Laura Gallant, for their dedication to maintaining the aesthetic and ideals of "Water of Whimsy" in the composition and format of this book. They were able to take the bits and pieces that I contributed, weaving them into a complete wonder.

I must acknowledge a debt of gratitude to my love and my light, Reid Ralston. Reid, my husband, has been a boon of support throughout all the work that went into this creation. Lastly, a thank-you to my parents, without whom none of this would have been possible.

ABOUT THE AUTHOR

Regan Ralston is a watercolor illustrator living in upstate New York with her husband, Reid and two lapdogs, Honey and Zuzu. She graduated from Indiana University with a Bachelor of Arts in English and completed courses at the State University of New York College at Cortland, pursuing a Master of Arts in Education.

Regan is a homespun artist, with most of her formal experience being gleaned from courses acquired during her pursuit of an art minor at university. Favoring folk art and cottage hewn aesthetics, Regan formalized her personal style over the past five years running her independent art shop Water of Whimsy. With a focus on lore, literature, history and magic, her art accentuates nostalgia and the ideals of storytelling.

Identifying as a modern-day Witch, Regan highlights aspects of neo-paganism and Wicca through her work and writing, celebrating key sabbats throughout the year and honoring seasonal changes in her art. Having popularized the idea of Witch types through her illustration series "Witch Aesthetics," Regan notes that she finds herself most aligned with the path of the Cottage and Kitchen Witch, savoring magic that comes from the heart of the home.

Index

Index

Index

Index